"Preaching has fallen on hard times. An open debate is now being waged over the character and centrality of preaching in the church. At stake is nothing less than the integrity of Christian worship and proclamation. In this book, Robby Gallaty and Steven Smith provide a biblically grounded manual for faithful proclamation of God's Word. Their commitment to the authority of Scripture and the centrality of preaching in the life of the church is a faithful witness in the age of entertainment-driven ministry. *Preaching for the Rest of Us* is a practical and theologically rich resource to help you grow in more faithful proclamation of God's Word."

—**R. Albert Mohler Jr.**, president,
The Southern Baptist Theological Seminary

"Robby Gallaty and Steven Smith have achieved something in *Preaching for the Rest of Us* that is genuinely unique. Recognizing the complication of much homiletical theory, these two great preachers have cobbled together a total introduction to preaching that is helpful to me! A grasp of the ultimate goal in preaching enables these prophets to walk all of us, beginner and established practitioner, down the highway of great biblical preaching. This is a significant contribution."

—**Paige Patterson**, president,
Southwestern Baptist Theological Seminary

"It wasn't until well into my pastoral ministry that I realized that we aren't going to fulfill the Great Commission solely with preachers like me—seminary-trained, vocational, and Westernized. It's going to take preachers who earn a living by their ministries and preachers who go to secular jobs every day. It's going to take preachers who've been to seminary and preachers who haven't. It's going to take preachers in America and preachers abroad. Gallaty and Smith get that. In *Preaching for the Rest of Us*, these two effective and experienced pastors 'put the cookies on the bottom shelf,' where all of us can grab and eat. They cull down the principles and processes of biblical exposition to the basic essentials. If you're looking for a trustworthy 'quick-start guide' (xvii) to preaching that's driven by both the theology and the text of Scripture, look no further."

—**Jim Shaddix**, W. A. Criswell Professor of Expository Preaching,
and director, Center for Pastoral Leadership and Preaching,
Southeastern Baptist Theological Seminary

PREACHING
FOR THE REST OF US

PREACHING
FOR THE REST OF US

ESSENTIALS
FOR
TEXT-DRIVEN
PREACHING

ROBBY GALLATY AND **STEVEN SMITH**

ACADEMIC

NASHVILLE, TENNESSEE

From Steven:

This book is lovingly dedicated to my parents,
Sandy and Bailey Smith.

Psalm 16:6

From Robby:

To Jim Shaddix:
From the first day I heard a text-driven sermon,
at Edgewater Baptist Church, until now,
my life and preaching have never been the same.
Thank you for modeling what you teach.

Contents

Acknowledgments

I (Steven) am very grateful to the many people who made this book a reality. Thank you to Daniel Dickard for heavy editing, for adding the discussion questions, and for many helpful conversations. Thank you also to Meagan Lacey for additional editing, and to Kyle Walker for reading an early draft and offering helpful comments. Thank you to Adam Malette for significant administrative support. I also need to thank Calvin Pearson. As lectures, these chapters grew out of early conversations when I was learning how to teach preaching. Calvin was an able mentor and a very gracious friend. Thanks also to David Allen, whose influence is throughout this book.

Thanks also to staff at Immanuel Baptist Church who read an early draft and offered comments: Brandon Watson, Matt Hubbard, and Adam Venters. Special thanks to Paige Patterson, who offered a sabbatical that helped me complete the manuscript. His personal influence is on most every page. Thanks also to my father-in-law, Ron Cherry, who put the idea for the book in my head and encouraged its completion.

Finally, I am most grateful for Team Smith: Ashley, who helped me think through so much of it conceptually, and of course, the Smithlings— Jewell, Sidney, and Shep. My favorite people in the world.

I (Robby) wouldn't be the preacher or the man I am today without God's calling and the Holy Spirit's power in my life. I've never gotten over what happened on November 12, 2002, the day God saved me.

Effective preaching is the result of both a diligent workman who prepares in the study and a congregation of people who come eager to hear from God. I am grateful to God for the three churches (Immanuel Baptist Church, Brainerd Baptist Church, and Long Hollow Baptist Church) I've had the privilege of pastoring and preaching to over the years.

I'm thankful that Steven reached out to partner together in this work. I've always appreciated his preaching and passion for God's Word, and it has been a joy to collaborate on this important topic.

I am also indebted to a few men who taught me the craft of text-driven preaching. Jim Shaddix modeled it weekly at Edgewater Baptist Church when I was a new believer before teaching me the basics in Proclaiming the Bible class at NOBTS. Reggie Ogea, Jerry Barlow, Don Wilton, and Dennis Phelps shaped my preaching through my doctoral studies. David Platt and Tony Merida not only taught me principles of expository preaching; they were a much-needed sounding board for refining my approach to the text and delivery of the Word. Tim Lafleur, over a summer in Glorieta, New Mexico, provided helpful insights as I prepared each week to preach to the one hundred students at the retreat center. Additionally, Mark Dever's constant encouragement to return to the Word of God for answers for church polity, preaching, and leadership fueled my passion to rely on the Word alone for life change.

I am grateful for the two-year weekly investment of John Fallahee, who selflessly served me as a new pastor at Brainerd Baptist Church. During our Monday meetings, I learned how to use Logos Bible software, the value of a feedback loop, and the importance of having preaching mentors post–seminary training. Finally, I'm thankful for my wife, Kandi's, constructive critiques after each week's sermons. You were not only helpful in constructing messages, but you also couched helpful comments in love after I delivered them. You have been a huge supporter of anything God leads me to do.

Preface

Leading a Text-Driven Life

*Now Ezra had determined in his heart to study the law of the LORD,
obey it, and teach its statutes and ordinances in Israel.*

—Ezra 7:10

Text-driven preaching flows from a text-driven life.

The text-driven sermon is not the big goal of life. Text-driven preaching is what happens when a preacher is so full of the text of Scripture that, when preached, the sermon represents the substance, structure, and spirit of the text. Art and calling imitate life. We defer to the text in the sermon because we defer to the text in all things. The sermon is simply a public working out of private conviction. The macro goal: to *live* a text-driven life. This commitment to knowing and doing the Word will, as Ezra modeled, lead to faithful teaching of the Word. The order is inviolable.

So, with all that needs to be said about preaching, and there is a lot, there are at least these overarching goals: to learn to love God through His Word and to lead others to do the same. The sermon, in its commitment to the Word, is a metaphor for life because the sermon is a reflection of how the life has been lived.

Loving God through His Word

Our love for preaching should be motivated by a love for God's Word—not in an academic sense, but rather, based on the reality that God has chosen to relate to us through His Word. This has always been true. From the Garden, God related to Adam and Eve through His spoken word (Genesis 1–3). God spoke to His people through His leaders Noah, Abraham, and Moses (Genesis–Deuteronomy). He codified His word in stone (Exodus 20) and then spoke to Israel through the prophets (Isaiah–Malachi). His Son, the Word, came to re-present His words to us as the final word (John 1:1–5; Heb 2:1–4). Then His Son ascended, leaving behind the Spirit, who would give witness to the Word (John 14:15–31). This Spirit is still actively making the complete Word come to life.

God's principal means of relating to us is His Word, illumined by His Spirit. God leads us through various means of grace, such as relationships, music, or circumstances. However, *His leading of us is always consistent with His revelation to us in Scripture.* Our fear is that the people we lead are far too busy looking for a word from God in places other than where His voice is clearly revealed: in His Word. We want the immediate, so we ignore the ultimate. We are called to lead God's people from this malaise to looking intently at His Word. *We want you to get into the Word until the Word gets into you.*

Leading People to His Word

This is the preacher's practice. We love God through His Word, and then we lead people to His Word. That's it. It's called "leading from the study." By this we mean the preacher commits to stay in the chair until the Word is clear, and as a result, the Word changes him. Then, watching the preacher change, the people also change as the Word activates their hearts. Eventually the listeners become leaders, who influence change in the church as well. At that point the pastor is leading the church from the study, from his willingness to stay in the seat until he knows what the text means. If the message doesn't move the preacher in the study, it probably won't move the people in the service.

God save us from loving preaching more than we love Scripture. God save us from loving expository preaching more than we love Scripture. The method is simply a means to the end of faithfulness to re-present what God has already spoken. Text-driven preaching is not the end. It is the means to the end of faithfulness. If at some point we find a method of preaching that more faithfully represents God's message than what we have presented in this book, we will quickly and gladly change our approach. In reality, change is the goal, a honing in the same direction. As our love for God's Word grows, we will find new ways to be more faithful to it. No methods are sacred. The method of text-driven preaching is valuable because it exalts what is sacred, God's Word, and it affirms in practice that we can do nothing but re-present it faithfully. We are not to give our lives to a method, but to figuring out the best way to present God's Word. Everything we do begins with a love for God's Word.

About Our Journey

Actually, both of us learned how to preach *after* seminary. This is an odd confession because we both had great formal educations; we learned from some of the best preaching professors and preachers. Yet after a few months of being pastors, we were struck by our own limitations. That's when our education began. My (Steve's) experience is that this is common. When you are learning something in the classroom, you just can't conceive of how it will play out in practice. It's in the practice that lectures finally make sense.

This is written for those who have not preached, for those who have no formal education, and for those who, like us, knew how to preach and later realized that it is more daunting than we originally imagined. If you got it all the first time in seminary, you may not need this book. This is preaching for the rest of us.

Whether you are just starting or restarting, we are grateful you have picked up this book. We have been on this journey and now are excited to serve you. So perhaps some introductions are in order.

We are from very different backgrounds and experiences. I grew up in a pastor's home, am a fourth-generation preacher, and was called to preach at an early age. I was a pastor for eight years, have taught preaching for the last 12 years, and have now transitioned back into the pastorate. Robby experienced a radical conversion to Christ after battling a three-year drug and alcohol addiction. He has been a pastor for the last 12 years.

We both have written books. Robby writes the kinds of books people want and need to read. I write the kinds of books that students have to read. And while I try, Robby will always have bigger biceps.

We share the same theological convictions and many of the same practices. However, we are different in the way we approach things and have tried to include this where appropriate. People who embrace the same high view of Scripture and therefore take preaching seriously still must tailor their approaches based on their personalities and contexts.

For me, this book puts to paper what I have been teaching for a while. Thus, much of what is here has already been said in a classroom, lecture, or blog. We've tried to give proper citation where possible, but I am fully aware that some, maybe many, thoughts have seeped in from other sources. The follow-up to this book, *Recapturing the Voice of God*, which explains how to preach the specific genres of Scripture, was written first, so we are grateful to Jim Baird and the team at B&H Academic for allowing some of that content to be reprinted here.

For Robby, this book conceptualizes the practices he has implemented for years as a pastor. By no means are we experts in text-driven preaching; however, we both share a passion to grow as preachers by remaining lifelong learners. We pray you share the same passion we do: correctly handling God's Word.

Why This Book?

The amount of literature on preaching makes another book seem presumptuous. However, we felt there was a place for a book that (1) taught text-driven preaching for those with no theological training, (2) was based on a theological foundation, and (3) was short.

There are thousands of volumes on preaching. This is a quick-start guide.

Our commitment is that we err on the side of being stripped down. This means we will leave out, or underemphasize, some important aspects of preaching. We encourage you to turn to the many resources that are available, and especially the Recommended Reading at the end of each chapter.

How to Use This Book

We want you to prepare a sermon as you are reading this book. Here's how:

Take your Bible, find a passage you want to preach, turn to chapter 3 in this book, and start working on it. Read each chapter and follow the steps. If you are not already, pretend you are a pastor working on a text to preach.

It might take time, so plan on two weeks to work on the sermon. At the end of two weeks, you will have a text-driven sermon. Can you learn to preach in two weeks? Of course not. But starting with the foundations might force you to ask why we would recommend something a certain way.

The disciplines here represent mountain peaks. In the same way that every mountain peak is supported by a mountain, there are theological and philosophical foundations that are not covered here. For that reason we have included two brief introductory chapters: an introduction to preaching and a theological foundation to preaching. Prayerfully looking at the peaks will make you want to climb the mountain, that is, to keep reading on preaching and expose yourself to the literature. Preaching is difficult. We need the motivation that comes from the conviction that God has revealed Himself in His Word.

So, let's begin on the wings of a prayer:

Lord, as we walk this road together, please help us fall in love with Your Word more deeply, and, as a result of loving You through Your Word, may we gladly submit to it. Then, as we work together, may

You give us the grace to then work out in a sermon the text You have worked into us. May we, like Ezra, who set his heart to study, do, and teach Your Word, do the same. In Jesus's name and for His glory. Amen.

Introduction

Throughout all of history—from creation to eternity, from Genesis to Revelation—God establishes His purposes through His word. Scripture echoes this truth, for at every turn the word of God does the work of God. In Genesis 1, the text repeatedly draws attention to God's speech: "God *said*, 'Let there be light'"; "God *said*, 'Let there be an expanse between the waters'"; and "God *said*, 'Let the water under the sky be gathered into one place'" (vv. 3, 6, 9). As we move through the Old Testament, we observe the word of God empowering men and women to do extraordinary things. We see the word of God come to Abraham in Genesis 12, and his obedience to it in the face of doubt and uncertainty is "credited to [him] for righteousness" (Rom 4:9).

We see the word of God come to Moses in a forgotten corner of the desert from a burning bush, telling him to approach the most powerful man in the world with a request to release God's people from captivity. Through Moses's obedience to this word, God's people are freed from centuries of slavery.

We see the word of God deliver commandments for this newly freed people to both sustain them as a nation and set them apart for their Creator's use. These commandments were so powerful that God commanded Moses's successor, "Above all, be strong and very courageous to carefully observe the whole instruction My servant Moses commanded you. Do not turn from it to the right or the left, so that you will have success wherever you go."[1]

---

[1] John R. W. Stott, *The Preacher's Portrait* (Grand Rapids: Eerdmans, 1961), 55.

1

We see the word of God come to ordinary men and turn them into prophets who proclaim the truth of God, no matter how difficult it is to hear or how much trouble it brings them. The word drives the speech of Isaiah: "Listen, heavens, and pay attention, earth, for the Lord has spoken" (Isa 1:2). It would not fail: "my word that comes from my mouth will not return to me empty, but it will accomplish what I please and will prosper in what I send it to do" (55:11). The same word comes to Ezekiel, whose book employs the phrase "The word of the Lord came to me" nearly 50 times. We also hear this phrase from Hosea, Joel, Amos, Micah, Zephaniah, Haggai, and Zechariah. We see it come to kings and peasants, to rulers and prophets and children. It guides a nation, restores severed bonds, penetrates the hearts of men, and rains down fire from the sky.

And then the word is silent for 400 years. But it is not dead, nor does it sleep.

Again we see the Word come from the mouth of John the Baptist as a "voice . . . crying out in the wilderness" (Matt 3:3; Mark 1:3). We are reminded that this word, which has saturated every facet of Scripture and history, has been constant since the beginning: "In the beginning was the Word, and the Word was with God, and the Word was God. He was with God in the beginning" (John 1:1–2). We learn that the Word created all things, both known and unknown, seen and invisible: "All things were created through him, and apart from him not one thing was created that has been created" (v. 3).

And then, most miraculously of all, we see for the first time the Word wrapped in flesh, cresting a hill to be baptized; and He is greeted with reverence and relief: "Here is the Lamb of God, who takes away the sin of the world!" (v. 29).

Paul instructed the Romans, "So faith comes from what is heard, and what is heard comes through the message about Christ" (Rom 10:17)— from hearing Scripture. In his final letter to Timothy, Paul emphasized the importance of studying the Word: "Be diligent to present yourself to God as one approved, a worker who doesn't need to be ashamed, correctly teaching the word of truth" (2 Tim 2:15). Likewise, the apostle Peter stated, "You have been born again—not of perishable seed but of imperishable—through the living and enduring word of God. For all flesh is like grass, and all its glory like a flower of the grass. The grass withers, and the flower falls, but the word of the Lord endures forever" (1 Pet 1:23–25). Jesus's half brother James, an unbeliever during Jesus's earthly ministry, penned these words years after his death: "By his own choice, *he gave us birth* by the word of truth so that we would be a kind of firstfruits of his creatures" (James 1:18).

The author of Hebrews cited the importance of the Word as well. At the outset of the book, the Word-made-flesh, Jesus Christ, is extolled as the Author of all things: "The Son is the radiance of God's glory and the exact expression of his nature, sustaining all things by his powerful word" (Heb 1:3). God's Word is described by its convicting nature: "For the word of God is living and effective and sharper than any double-edged sword, penetrating as far as the separation of soul and spirit, joints and marrow. It is able to judge the thoughts and intentions of the heart" (4:12).

It is no wonder that the Mishnah, a collection of the Jewish traditions, encourages followers of God to "pore over it [the Scripture] again and again, for everything is contained in it; look into it, grow old and gray over it, and do not depart from it, for there is no better pursuit for you than this."[2] Every instance of effective preaching throughout Scripture is nothing but a proclamation of God's Word.[3] Even today, the Word is not an archaic device used in an ancient text; it is alive and breathing and working actively, and it is a preacher's job to deliver it appropriately. The purpose of this book is to help equip preachers, and anyone else who shares the Word of the Lord, to do it correctly, appropriately, and with the respect it deserves.

---

[2] Mishnah, Pirke Avot 5:27; Ann Spangler and Lois Tverberg, *Sitting at the Feet of Rabbi Jesus: How the Jewishness of Jesus Can Transform Your Faith* (Grand Rapids: Zondervan, 2009), loc. 4183, Kindle.

[3] Robby Gallaty, *Firmly Planted* (Nashville: B&H, 2015), 6–8.

The Word Does the Work

Charles Spurgeon, the so-called prince of preachers, declared, "Nobody ever outgrows Scripture: the book widens and deepens with our years."[4] When a man steps behind the sacred desk, he stands on the shoulders of generations of faithful men who have come before him. The task of preaching supersedes all other ministry assignments, for the calling is not to speak merely about God, but to be a mouthpiece for God, saying, "Thus says the Lord." The task requires a supernatural anointing from on high. Jesus's first recorded message in His hometown synagogue began with His reading of the words, "The Spirit of the Lord is on me, because he has anointed me to preach good news" (Luke 4:18).

The journey toward dividing the Word of God with accuracy begins with understanding the Bible's authority. The pulpit's power does not come through cute stories, funny illustrations, or carefully crafted outlines. It comes from the exposition of God's Word. Paul challenged his son in the faith, Timothy, like this: "I solemnly charge you before God and Christ Jesus, who is going to judge the living and the dead, and because of his appearing and his kingdom: *Preach the word*" (2 Tim 4:1–2). R. Kent Hughes explains:

> [Jesus's] *logos*, his word, was perfect. Whatever he said was absolutely true. His exegesis of Scripture was flawless. His application of spiritual truth was the most penetrating in all of history, as we see in such discourses as the Sermon on the Mount.
>
> His *ethos*, the kind of person he was, was without parallel in the human race. The tone of his voice, the expression on his face, the integrity of his eyes flowed with truth. His *pathos* came from a heart absolutely convinced of man's need, absolutely loving, and absolutely determined. There never has been anyone as truly passionate as Christ in all human experience.

---

[4] Charles Spurgeon, *The Complete Works of Charles Spurgeon*, vol. 17, *Sermons 968 to 1027* (1871; n.p.: DelMarva, 2013), Kindle.

These three, his *logos*, *ethos*, and *pathos*, blended in Christ with such force that he, from the beginning, was the greatest communicator the world has ever known![5]

Jesus, as the walking Word of God, should be our example for preaching the Word of God. To do this correctly, certain presuppositions should be fundamental for preachers:

- Scripture is *inspired*, or the breath of God (2 Tim 3:16–17)
- Scripture is *inerrant*, or without errors (John 17:17).
- Scripture is *infallible*, or will not lead us astray (1 Pet 1:23–25).
- Scripture is *sufficient*, or all we need for salvation (Rom 10:13–15, 17).

Another crucial point is that preaching itself is an act of extending grace to listeners.

Grace to You

Have you ever noticed that Paul introduced his letters with the words, "Grace to you," and ended many of them the same way? Examples of this can be found in Galatians and Ephesians. Galatians begins with "Grace to you and peace from God the Father and our Lord Jesus Christ" (1:3), and ends with "Brothers and sisters, the grace of our Lord Jesus Christ be with your spirit. Amen" (6:18). Ephesians begins with "Grace to you and peace from God our Father and the Lord Jesus Christ" (1:2), and closes with "Grace be with all who have undying love for our Lord Jesus Christ" (6:24). The same turn of phrase can be seen to some degree in almost all of Paul's writings.

Indeed, grace accompanies the Word of God. Paul literally bookended his words with it. God freely gives grace to us, and preachers can extend grace to their hearers through the proclamation of God's Word.

---

[5] R. Kent Hughes, *Mark: Jesus, Servant and Savior*, 2 vols. in 1, ESV ed. (Wheaton, IL: Crossway, 2015), chap. 4.

Begin with the End in Mind

At the very core, every disciple of Jesus is to be a student for life. In the same vein, becoming an effective communicator of God's Word is a lifelong journey. This book is going to delve into a number of areas that will sharpen your skills as a preacher, but many of them will not be easy to implement. Preaching the Word of God requires dedication and complete removal of yourself from the equation. The moment your sermon becomes about you is the moment you must take serious stock of where you stand as a preacher.

Miss Betty's comment after every sermon, "Pastor, that was the best sermon I've ever heard," may be comforting, but it is not very helpful in a preacher's journey of developing into a better communicator of God's Word. Opening up a sermon to critique can be tough at first, but it is an essential step for growth. Constructive criticism is necessary for development, and it can only come through humility. Trusted friends and staff members can be some of your greatest assets in becoming a better preacher.

Every preacher needs a feedback loop. This can take place over coffee, breakfast, or dinner. Do you have trustworthy, faithful men in your church who can meet once a week? Are there students you can meet with who sense a leading into ministry? Are there Sunday school teachers you can meet with once a week? Maybe you can gather with other pastors in the area to talk about ways to progress as a preacher.

Equally debilitating to the growth of a preacher is laziness. As this book will reveal, expository preaching is hard work, which may be why many default back to easier methods that often lead to doctrinal error.

Let this not be said of us. The same Spirit who can empower in the pulpit can anoint in the study. A systematic process of preparation curbs laziness. As it is often quipped (in one variation or another), "If you fail to plan, you can plan to fail."

Let's continue our journey together by establishing a theology of preaching.

1 | A Theology of Text-Driven Preaching

There is no shortage of good arguments for preaching in an expository, text-driven way. Perhaps the most significant argument stems from the nature of the Word itself. If we believe Scripture contains the very words of God and that both God and what He speaks are perfect, then anything we do that hinders our presenting Scripture is a tragedy. While the nature of the Word is the primary factor that compels expositional preaching, the nature of the preacher's call and the nature of the church also lend support to this methodology. These three arguments for text-driven preaching may be summarized as follows:

1. The Nature of the Word: *We are called to preach Christ, and Christ is revealed in the Word.*
2. The Nature of the Call: *Preaching the text is working out our own call to ministry by crucifying our personal agendas so others might live, and thus living according to Christ's example.*
3. The Nature of the Church: *The Word of God sanctifies the church.*

After we deal with these three axioms, we will deal with the nature of text-driven preaching.

The Nature of the Word: We Are Called to Preach Christ, and Christ Is Revealed in the Word

Nothing is clearer from the biblical witness than that the apostles were consumed with preaching Christ. He, and He alone, was their message. Notice in a few sample texts how simple the apostles' message was:

> [Peter and John] were teaching the people and *proclaiming in Jesus the resurrection of the dead.* (Acts 4:1–2)

> Every day in the temple, and in various homes, they continued teaching and proclaiming *the good news that Jesus is the Messiah.* (Acts 5:42)

> Some of them . . . began speaking to the Greeks also, proclaiming *the good news about the Lord Jesus.* (Acts 11:20)

> "This *Jesus I am proclaiming to you is the Messiah."* (Acts 17:3)

> "But *we preach Christ . . ."* (1 Cor 1:23)

> "For we are not proclaiming ourselves but *Jesus Christ as Lord."* (2 Cor 4:5)

> "God . . . was pleased to reveal his Son in me, *so that I could preach him . . ."* (Gal 1:16)

Luke references the preaching of Christ interchangeably with the preaching of the Word (see Acts 8:4; 13:3). To the biblical authors, preaching Christ meant preaching the message of His death, burial, and resurrection, and all it implies. To say we "preach Jesus" implies both proclamation and explanation. We are proclaiming Christ and saying about Him what God has said about Him.

The first preachers were making a massive theological claim when they preached that Jesus was "the Messiah," or, the Christ (Acts 5:42). The significance of this cannot be overstated. We must remember that for hundreds of years, the Jews had been looking for their promised Messiah. They expected a warrior like David to liberate them from bondage, to restore Israel to the kingdom it once was. Yet Scripture spoke of a suffering Messiah (Isa 52:13–53:12). Paul made this clear in 1 Cor 15:1–4:

> Now I want to make clear for you, brothers and sisters, the gospel I preached to you, which you received, on which you have taken your stand and by which you are being saved, if you hold to the message I preached to you—unless you believed in vain. For I passed on to you as most important what I also received: that Christ died for our sins according to the Scriptures, that he was buried, that he was raised on the third day *according to the Scriptures*.

Paul's point here was that Christ's actions had been prophesied in the Old Testament. Therefore, Paul argued, Jesus must be the Christ because His life fit the prophesied pattern. We also see in Acts 5:42 and 17:3 that the first Christians were Jews trying to make this connection as they preached. Jesus was, and is, the Christ.

The passage just referenced in 1 Corinthians, in addition to announcing Jesus as Messiah, also functions in another way: it interprets Old Testament texts. Since Paul believed the Old Testament revelation of Christ validated the New Testament appearance of Christ, he did what Jesus had done during His time on earth: he opened the Old Testament and explained its teaching about Christ.

We have an odd tendency to reverse this in our preaching. We stick to the New Testament and disregard the majority of our Bibles. Often, the reasoning for such a practice is that the Old Testament is strange and foreign, separated from us by years and continents and history. However, did you ever stop to think that when the apostles were "preaching Jesus" they were interpreting the Old Testament?

We can't love Jesus without a practical love of God's Word. Additionally, we won't be able to fully appreciate the New Testament until we understand the Old Testament. The Bible is God's chosen means to help us comprehend

Christ, and Christ is the One who helps us understand the Bible. These two ideas are crucial if we are to preach in a way that honors Him.

Scripture Reveals Christ

It is clear the New Testament is about Christ. The first four books reveal His actions, the book of Acts reveals the work of His church immediately after His ascension, the Epistles outline how He leads His church, and the New Testament concludes with Christ revealed.

However, the New Testament is not merely *about* Christ; Christ *inspired* it (2 Tim 3:16) and prepared His disciples to receive it. In John 16:12, Jesus said to His disciples, "I still have many things to tell you, but you can't bear them now." What were these things He would later say? They were the books of Romans through Revelation: the rest of the New Testament. The Scriptures that were not spoken directly from the mouth of Jesus during His earthly ministry are still His words. The New Testament is the early church working out Christ's teaching.

In John 16, Jesus made another remarkable statement. He said that by the authority of Christ, the Holy Spirit would reveal truth to the church: "When the Spirit of truth comes, he will guide you into all the truth. For he will not speak on his own, but he will speak whatever he hears. He will also declare to you what is to come. He will glorify me, because he will take from what is mine and declare it to you" (vv. 13–14).

Here we learn that Jesus is the mind behind the New Testament. And since He ascended to heaven before the New Testament was written, the Holy Spirit revealed these things and, in so doing, glorified Jesus. The Bible is Jesus teaching us about Jesus. Every time we open the pages of Scripture and read, the Holy Spirit speaks to us what Jesus would tell us if He were physically with us. Scripture is a living Word, which exhales the very presence of Christ. It gives glory to Christ. Christ is the Word, and there is no knowledge of Him without the inscripturated Word.

Remarkably, preaching is an act that involves the entire Trinity. As we explain the Word of God, the Holy Spirit draws attention to Jesus, who always gives glory to the Father. This realization is breathtaking in its simplicity and electrifying in its reality. Imagine it: a triune God, working through a preacher who is redeemed by His blood and conformed to the image of His Son, delivering His Word to bring Himself glory. You might want to stop here and praise Him. This reality is hardly comprehensible.

Ultimately, the New Testament is inspired *by* Christ, it is given to us *through* Christ, and it is written to draw attention *to* Christ as He *is glorified* in us.

But preaching Christ from the New Testament is the easier part of our task, because Christ's name is literally written all over the 27 books. It may seem a bit surprising, especially for a twenty-first-century Christian, that the entirety of the Old Testament is about Him as well.

Scripture Reveals Christ in the Old Testament

To say that we can see Christ in the Old Testament is not to suggest Jesus is embedded either physically or figuratively in every Old Testament narrative, law, poem, and prophecy. The Old Testament is, instead, a narrative that meanders through time and continents, pointing always toward its climax: the New Testament's revelation of Jesus, the Messiah, who redeems His bride and defeats His enemies. The Old Testament is a prelude to a Person. It leads us to the fulfillment of God's promises in Christ.

Consider Luke 24:27. When walking with two of His disciples, Jesus began with "Moses, and all the Prophets," and He "interpreted for them the things concerning himself in all the Scriptures." This is a remarkable passage because those disciples saw for the first time the hermeneutic of God. God did not just tweak their thoughts. He taught them a whole new way to read the Old Testament. It was—and is—to be understood as an introduction. A prelude. A book intended to whet the appetite for things yet to come.

When Jesus explained to those disciples how to read the Old Testament, it revolutionized the way His followers thought. We see the result of their expositional study of the Old Testament in the very first Christian sermon, when Peter stood up and explained Jesus from three Old Testament texts: Joel 2, Psalm 16, and Psalm 110. We can only assume that after hearing Jesus explain Himself from the Old Testament, the disciples' newfound hermeneutic gave them a new way of preaching. They had personally experienced Him but were still preaching Christ from the Old Testament!

The point is clear: All Scripture has a storyline we might call "salvation history." Salvation history has its apex in the incarnation, death, and resurrection of Christ and its consummation in the book of Revelation when God makes all things right.

As we read the Bible, Jesus, the Word incarnate, teaches us about Himself. If we skip around the Bible, gleaning snippets of truth here and there without ever grasping the big picture, we will never understand what Jesus wants us to know about Himself. This truth is both scary and tragic.

PREACHING JESUS

One rebuttal to an expositional method of preaching may come from a preacher who says he "just preaches Jesus" rather than delving into the nuances of specific Scripture passages. But how do we know who Jesus is apart from Scripture? If we do not know Scripture, then we really do not know Jesus—if you do not know the Word of God, you cannot know the God of the Word. We must not mistake a call to healthy simplicity for a misguided call to simplemindedness. If someone is proclaiming Christ without explaining Scripture, then where are they getting their picture of Christ? The vision of Christ that is presented must be reinvented from a source besides Scripture. In other words, if we don't learn who Christ is from Scripture, where else will we learn who Christ is? Aberrant theology grows when a pulpit is not seeding the Word. On the other hand, explaining Scripture is the God-ordained means to produce spiritual fruit (Matt 13:23).

To preach Jesus without preaching Scripture is to preach a Jesus we do not know. If Scripture is the means God chose to reveal Himself, then the message of Christ is only significant if it is tethered to the Scriptures. To say that we love Jesus but not the Bible is an exercise in self-delusion. If it were not for Scripture, we would never know that Jesus:

- is the great Shepherd over His sheep (Heb 13:20)
- hates when people twist Scripture (Luke 16:16–17)
- brings a truth that will divide families (Luke 12:49–53)
- seeks sinners (Luke 15–16)
- asks complete allegiance from His followers (Luke 9:23–27, 57–62)
- wants to spend time with us (Luke 10:38–41)
- calls us to pray boldly (Luke 11:5–13)

Without the Scriptures, you cannot understand who Christ is in the meaningful way God intended.

We are called to preach the message of Christ. To do so, we must understand what that message is. Not one person has ever become a Christian without hearing the Word of God—for how can they believe in Him of whom they have not heard (see Rom 10:14)? Beyond this, there is no meaningful growth in Christ without Scripture, for it is the very Word of God. Preaching that facilitates godly growth is preaching that takes care to explain Scripture. We preach the Bible because the Bible reveals Christ.

The Nature of the Call: Christ Calls Us to Die So Others Might Live

Preachers often struggle with self-perception. Are we to be like Billy Graham, calling masses to immediate response? Are we to be psychologists, working people through their personal problems? Are we simply to be communicators, trying to get ideas into our congregants' minds? Are we to be personifications of trendiness to show that God is relevant?

The internal struggle for pastoral identity has more to do with theology than it does cultural shifts. Consider how the apostle Paul described his identity as a preacher in 2 Cor 4:7–12:

> Now we have this treasure in clay jars, so that this extraordinary power may be from God and not from us. We are afflicted in every way but not crushed; we are perplexed but not in despair; we are persecuted but not abandoned; we are struck down but not destroyed. We always carry the death of Jesus in our body, so that the life of Jesus may also be displayed in our body. For we who live are always being given over to death for Jesus's sake, so that Jesus's life may also be displayed in our mortal flesh. So then, death is at work in us, but life in you.

Paul's ambition was the Corinthians' spiritual health. To effect their growth he knew he must die to his own agenda and extend Christ to them. Knowing that preaching is dying to self so others might live curtails a preacher's inclination to please people or seek self-fulfillment. Many preachers' perpetual image management may be direr than it appears on the surface. We suspect it belies an insecurity that actually repels the unredeemed.

Christ died for us. We die for the people. This is our identity without reservation or hesitation. There is no unexposed corner to which we can retreat. Our will is lost in Christ's. The preacher of Christ is nothing but a tool that Christ uses to bring about His plans. We cannot save people, but we can labor—and suffer—for their sanctification. So, we surrender our wills to the One who surrendered His life to the Father. Through His death, people live. Through His suffering, congregations heal.

When we surrender our lives to the One who surrendered His life for us, we join Him in death and suffering—death to selfish ambition and the suffering that accompanies that path. Christ's death wasn't painless; it was a crucifixion. Neither will the preacher's death to self be painless. The crucified preacher is the template by which all preaching should be measured. Some may use the pulpit as a place to illustrate what great preachers they are, to work out personal angst, to push a political agenda, or simply to vent. However, to use the pulpit in such a way is to treat it as a platform. But it's not a platform. It's a cross. Therefore, the best metaphor for preaching the gospel is the gospel itself: We are dead to self and raised to life in Christ, preaching a message of death to life in Christ so others might live.[1]

Preaching can be a platform to dispense advice, a venue to help people with marital or financial problems, or an activity to arouse public opinion or engage the culture. While sermons can be used to do these things, if these things become their purpose, we have missed the function of the pulpit: to dispense the Word of God. Using the pulpit for these activities alone demonstrates a misunderstanding of how God's Word functions in the life of the believer and the church. Therefore, we must next explain how the Word is to function in the life of the church.

The Nature of the Church: The Word of God Sanctifies the Believer

Water is powerful. A docile lake or a peaceful ocean may seem tranquil and harmless, but if we unleash a dam or allow a river to run over its banks, we witness the raw power of water. The Word of God is equally powerful—a mighty, rushing river. Though, like water, it appears tranquil at times, we are tempted to view the Word as a book that is kind and gentle. Approaching it as little more than a self-help manual is to overlook its raw, unfathomable power.

Our ambition is not to dip into the Word and sprinkle people with doses of truth. Rather, we want to unleash the dam by fully immersing people in the Word of God. One reason we preach Scripture is because God designed it to be the means by which He sanctifies His people. Let's briefly look at three truths about the Word of God.

---

[1] Steven W. Smith, *Dying to Preach: Embracing the Cross in the Pulpit* (Grand Rapids: Kregel, 2009).

1. *The function of the Word of God in the lives of believers is to conform them to Christ's image.* In John 15:1–3, Jesus tells His disciples, "I am the true vine, and my Father is the gardener. Every branch in me that does not produce fruit he removes, and he prunes every branch that produces fruit so that it will produce more fruit. You are already clean because of the word I have spoken to you."

2. Here we see a unique function of the words of Christ: *they perform a verbal pruning.* Hearing and obeying the words of Christ requires acknowledging where we fall short of God's expectations and allowing Him to cut out harmful behaviors and attitudes. When we preach, we should be preaching Scripture, because Scripture alone has power to shape a person into the image of Christ and make him or her more effective at producing spiritual fruit.

3. *Thus, the more of the Word God's people hear, the more they will be like Christ.* How much they mirror Christ is proportionate to the amount of Scripture to which they are exposed. This is not absorption of dry exegesis. Rather, this is hungry consumption of the revelation of Jesus Christ through His Word, preached with boldness, compassion, force, and clarity. This Word is the agent the Holy Spirit uses for sanctification. Think of it this way: if the Spirit is the fire, the Word is the fuel. The more a believer is fueled by intake of God's Word, the hotter he or she will burn for Christ.

4. *What is true of a believer individually is true of the church corporately.* In Paul's comparison of marriage to the gospel, he encourages men, "Husbands, love your wives, just as Christ loved the church and gave himself for her to make her holy, cleansing her with the washing of water by the word" (Eph 5:25–26). The husband is commanded to prepare his wife to meet her ultimate groom: Christ. This preparation is modeled for the husband in the way Christ makes His own bride, the church, pure by washing her with the Word.

Preaching may accomplish many things, but its main function in the life of the believer individually and the church corporately is to shape us into the image of Christ. Any approach to preaching that aims for something different misses the point. The Word of God can help me with my problems, fix my marriage, and straighten out my finances. Those are important issues, but they are superficial compared to the ultimate goal of bringing glory to God by being shaped into the image of His Son. All those things can be a part of our sanctification, but that is just it: they are a *part*, not the whole. Christ is sanctifying us through His Word. Therefore, the ultimate aim of our preaching should be to bring every aspect of our lives into conformity to His.

So the question becomes something more personal: How can this sanctifying work occur in the people if it does not first occur in the preacher? How can the people live to Christ and die to self if the pulpit illustrates (verbally or nonverbally) that the preacher is very much alive to self? If the pulpit is a showcase for the preacher, how can people abandon their flesh and die to self?

The answer is, they can't. We are back to Paul's understanding of ministry. As we die, the people live. Puritan preacher Richard Baxter once said, "I preached as a dying man to dying men."[2] We suffer so they will thrive. This is the biblical understanding of ministry, and a biblical understanding of preaching. Still, someone might ask the question: where in the Bible does it say that we have to preach text-driven sermons? This is a good question.

Is Text-Driven Preaching Biblical?[3]

Is there a text in Scripture that defends this method? It would be tempting to answer with a reference to Paul's simple "Preach the Word" in 2 Tim 4:2. However, while Paul's admonition to Timothy is clear enough, it is a charge to explain Christ from all of Scripture more than it is a defense of

---

[2] Richard Baxter, *The Reformed Pastor* (Edinburgh: Banner of Truth Trust, 1656; 2007), 174.

[3] This section is adapted from Steven Smith's *Recapturing the Voice of God: Shaping Sermons Like Scripture* (Nashville: B&H Academic, 2015).

text-driven preaching. Citing it as an apologetic for text-driven preaching would be to ignore all the magnificent things it *is* saying!

The truth of the matter is that a simple proof text does not exist. The reason we wave the banner of text-driven preaching is not because of one isolated text. Text-driven preaching is a theologically driven philosophy of homiletics based on the implications of numerous biblical passages.

The rationale for text-driven preaching is found through answering a question: is it the pastor's responsibility to explain Scripture to his congregation? Our stance is clear, but before we explain ourselves, let us first note that many pastors seem to pick a weekly topic to address in light of Scripture rather than allow Scripture to inform their congregations. To answer our question, we could look at numerous sections of Scripture, but for brevity's sake let's restrict our search to Paul's words to Timothy and Titus in the Pastoral Epistles, since they explicitly deal with the role and function of a pastor. Look at this collection of verses from 1 and 2 Timothy and Titus:

> Remain in Ephesus, so that you may instruct certain people not to teach false doctrine. (1 Tim 1:3)

> An overseer, therefore, must be . . . able to teach. (1 Tim 3:2)

> If you point these things out to the brothers and sisters, you will be a good servant of Christ Jesus, nourished by the words of the faith and the good teaching that you have followed. (1 Tim 4:6)

> Command and teach these things. (1 Tim 4:11)

> Until I come, give your attention to public reading, exhortation, and teaching. (1 Tim 4:13)

> Pay close attention to your life and your teaching; persevere in these things, for in doing this you will save both yourself and your hearers. (1 Tim 4:16)

> Command this also, so that they will be above reproach. (1 Tim 5:7)

Publicly rebuke those who sin, so that the rest will be afraid. (1 Tim 5:20)

Teach and encourage these things. If anyone teaches false doctrine and does not agree with the sound teaching of our Lord Jesus Christ and with the teaching that promotes godliness, he is conceited and understands nothing, but has an unhealthy interest in disputes and arguments over words. From these come envy, quarreling, slander, evil suspicions, and constant disagreement among people whose minds are depraved and deprived of the truth, who imagine that godliness is a way to material gain. (1 Tim 6:2–5)

Hold on to the pattern of sound teaching that you have heard from me. (2 Tim 1:13)

What you have heard from me in the presence of many witnesses, commit to faithful men who will be able to teach others also. (2 Tim 2:2)

Remind them of these things, and charge them before God not to fight about words. (2 Tim 2:14)

Be diligent to present yourself to God as one approved, a worker who doesn't need to be ashamed, correctly teaching the word of truth. (2 Tim 2:15)

So if anyone purifies himself from anything dishonorable, he will be a special instrument, set apart, useful to the Master, prepared for every good work. (2 Tim 2:21)

But as for you, continue in what you have learned and firmly believed. You know those who taught you, and you know that from infancy you have known the sacred Scriptures. (2 Tim 3:14–15)

All Scripture is inspired by God and is profitable for teaching, for rebuking, for correcting, for training in righteousness . . . (2 Tim 3:16)

I solemnly charge you before God and Christ Jesus, who is going to
judge the living and the dead, and because of his appearing and his
kingdom: Preach the word; be ready in season and out of season;
rebuke, correct, and encourage with great patience and teaching.
(2 Tim 4:1–2)

. . . holding to the faithful message as taught, so that he will be able
both to encourage with sound teaching and to refute those who
contradict it. (Titus 1:9)

But you are to proclaim things consistent with sound teaching.
(Titus 2:1)

From these texts alone, no matter what else Paul expected Timothy and
Titus to do, it is clear he at the very least expected them to explain the
Word of God to the people. This handful of passages from three relatively
short books contains more than a dozen admonitions to explain the truth of
Scripture. If we couple this with Paul's statements about protecting revealed
truth (1 Tim 1:11; 6:20; 2 Tim 1:12, 14), the case is even stronger for
the responsibility of pastors to explain the truth of Scripture to the people.
Someone is responsible for explaining the Word of God in any gathering
intended to draw people closer to the God of the Word.

Now that a case has been made for the pastor's role as a Scripture expositor, expository preaching is the only answer to this question. Text-driven
preaching is not a style; it is a theologically driven philosophy of preaching.
It is a method that facilitates a mandate.

Conclusion

In the following chapters we will discuss the nuts and bolts of preparing
a text-driven sermon. But it was essential to lay a foundation for the why
behind the how before proceeding. This may sound odd, but this book is
not calling you to embrace a methodology. Methodologies will change from
time to time. And they should. What we are committed to is the simple

belief that God has revealed Himself in Scripture and that we need to adopt the method that best allows us to share His revelation.

What follows is a template that helps us faithfully live out our theology and is a good method only insomuch as it is faithful to our theology of preaching.

So, what is a text-driven sermon?

Discussion Questions

1. If the Word is the agent used by the Holy Spirit for sanctification, how does this impact our view of Scripture and, ultimately, our theology of preaching?
2. Text-driven preaching is a philosophy that emanates from a high view of Scripture. How does this philosophy of preaching influence our method of preaching?
3. Read Luke 24:27. Luke records Jesus revealing Himself through the Old Testament Scriptures. How does this verse, specifically, impact a theology of preaching?
4. The preacher dies so that others may live. How does this manifest itself on a week-to-week basis for preachers?

Recommended Reading

Adam, Peter. *Speaking God's Word: A Practical Theology of Expository Preaching.* Downers Grove, IL: InterVarsity Press, 1996.

Akin, Daniel L., David L. Allen, and Ned L. Matthews. *Text Driven Preaching: God's Word at the Heart of Every Sermon.* Nashville: B&H Academic, 2010.

Litfin, Duane. *Paul's Theology of Preaching: The Apostle's Challenge to the Art of Persuasion in Ancient Corinth.* Downers Grove, IL: InterVarsity Press, 2015.

MacArthur, John, Jr. *Rediscovering Expository Preaching: Balancing the Science and Art of Biblical Exposition.* Nashville: Thomas Nelson, 1992.

Meyer, Jason C. *Preaching: A Biblical Theology.* Wheaton: IL, Crossway, 2013.

Smith, Steven W. *Dying to Preach: Embracing the Cross in the Pulpit.* Grand Rapids: Kregel, 2009.

2 | What Is Text-Driven Preaching?[1]

Preaching is more than explaining Scripture, but it's certainly not less. The purpose of this book is to teach a method that will allow the preacher to explain or exposit a text of Scripture in the sermon. The method of preaching that faithfully accomplishes this is often called *expository, expositional,* or *text-driven* preaching. The three terms will be used interchangeably. Since "expositional preaching" can mean many things to many people, it would help to begin with a discussion of what it is not.

> *Text-driven preaching is not an exegetical Bible study.* Some preachers tend to use the pulpit to bring to light many fascinating nuances of a text. The biblical text *is* fascinating. However, a majority of what we uncover in the study will never make it to the pulpit. The point of the pulpit, ultimately, is not information but transformation. We dispense the Word so the Spirit will work in the lives of our congregation.

> *Text-driven preaching is not a heavily outlined sermon.* Sometimes a weighty outline, with points and subpoints, is a fair representation

---

[1] A version of this chapter originally appeared in Smith's *Recapturing the Voice of God* (see chap 1, n. 3).

of the structure of the text. But the preacher searching for points is tempted to extract points from the text that do not accurately represent its message. Sometimes—most times—the text is simpler than three points. Sometimes it is more complicated. While a thick outline may occasionally be needed, we are not advocating outlining for the sake of outlining. The text itself will determine the structure of the outline.

Text-driven preaching is not necessarily preaching "verse by verse." Some believe they are doing text-driven, expository preaching simply because they are preaching consecutively through books of the Bible. However, it is possible to preach consecutively through a book and never get the point of the individual passages within the book. Likewise, it is possible to preach on a topic using individual passages, and miss the context for which they were intended. Merely working through a text without proper context is a pitfall to be avoided.

The preacher preparing an expositional sermon must remember that many suppositions about expositional preaching, and even Scripture itself, are incorrect. Since much exposition is done sequentially through a text, an easy mistake is to adhere rigidly to a set number of verses for each sermon. It is important to remember that chapter and verse divisions were added long after the text was written. The text, not the verse structure, is inspired. Here are two other misconceptions about expositional preaching:

An expositional sermon is a boring sermon. A boring sermon is most certainly not a text-driven sermon. Since neither the text of Scripture nor the truth it contains is boring, a sermon that accurately reflects the text cannot bore a Spirit-filled listener. If I preach a boring sermon, it's on me. God is not boring. When He speaks, it is not boring. A sermon that is boring does not accurately present what is going on in the text.

An expositional sermon is a confusing sermon. Scripture can be complicated. However, the purpose of Scripture is to reveal God, not conceal Him. A sermon that confuses people often comes from a preacher who has not done the hard work of making the text clear. Whatever else a sermon does, it should provide clarity by explaining the single point of the text. In this sense, all text-driven sermons are topical sermons; the text-driven sermon simply lets the text determine the topic.

So, what is expository, text-driven preaching?

Text-driven preaching is the interpretation and communication of a biblical text in a sermon that re-presents the substance, structure, and the spirit of the text.

Before we unpack this definition let's look at what it *does not* include.

Reading things into the text that are not there. There is a problem if a preacher says, "I have my idea. I just don't have a text to go with it." Having a great sermon idea and then finding a text to support it opens up the possibility of forcing a text into a box where it does not fit. As believers, and most certainly as preachers, we shouldn't come up with ideas and then search for texts to justify them. We are to be in the Word until it speaks through us. We shouldn't just study the Bible to preach. We should preach because we've studied the Bible. The Word flows out of our time spent with the Lord. God's Word is not to be our megaphone. We are to be its megaphone. It is our task to re-present what God has said.

Emphasizing the second- or third-level of meaning of a text as if it were the primary meaning. Oftentimes a sermon that follows this model will use a text completely out of its context. Other times it will take an application of a text and treat it as if it were the text's primary meaning. Occasionally, there is a place for expositing the second- and third-level meanings of a text when preaching a passage and wanting to show connections throughout Scripture. But this is an exception that should not become our rule.

So, let's focus on what this definition *does* mean by highlighting each of the keywords it contains.

Interpretation

In the process of interpretation, we answer the question, "What does this text mean?" To answer this question, we study the text in the original language using all the exegetical tools at our disposal—not to flex our research muscles or our superb grasp of ancient languages, but for the sole purpose of understanding what the text means. I (Robby) rarely mention the Greek or Hebrew word in a sermon unless it is transliterated into English. An example of this would be the Greek word *gumnazo*, which is where we get the English word *gymnasium* (see 1 Tim. 4:7, where it is translated "train"). Typically, interpreting a text correctly should constitute half of the pastor's sermon preparation time; however, there are exceptions to this rule of thumb because some passages demand more time than others for accurate interpretation.

The temptation, of course, is to shortcut this process: to try to figure out *how* to communicate the text before we know *what* the text actually communicates. It is possible to find a way to say something before we figure out what the text says, but this is a dangerous way to approach the Word of God. *Remember: we are not preaching sermons; we are preaching texts.* We are re-presenting what God has already said. Speechmaking is not difficult; re-presenting the Word of God is. The secret of "great" preaching is often found in staying at the task until the meaning of the text is clear. So, the first part of preaching is the interpretation of the text. The end result of this process is an exegetical outline—the raw ingredients of the sermon, but not yet ready to preach.

Getting Closer by Stepping Back

When preparing a sermon, it is easy to get stuck wondering what a text means, even after years of preparing text-driven sermons. Sometimes this kind of roadblock appears because we haven't spent enough time in the Scripture.

Yet not every case of interpretation block is caused by lack of study. In fact, when many of us reach this kind of block, our response is to dig in and study *harder*. We put in more hours on the passage, zoom the lens in as tight as possible to see every nuance in focus, and still don't feel confident we know what the text means. One reason for this is that sometimes the meaning of the text is not in the words alone. We may have to look for the meaning of the text in its surroundings. I (Steven) personally experienced this solution while trying to interpret the difficult parable of the rich man and Lazarus in Luke 16:19–31. I studied the text but could not get a good handle on what it was saying. So, I honed my focus and dug into the semantic structure of the sentences and the meaning of the individual words. And yet, the more I drilled down, the further I got from the meaning of the text. What I needed was to pan out.

If you pan out to the previous chapter, you see that the parable is the last of five parables dealing with lostness (15:1–16:31): four positive examples followed by a negative one. In the first four, Jesus was painting a picture of how He views lostness—He seeks people and loves them more than anything. Then He chastised the Pharisees for loving money and tampering with the Word of God (16:14–18) and shared the story of a man who loved money more than he loved people (16:19–20) and who had a low view of Scripture (16:27–31). That wide-angle view helped me realize that this provocative parable, which includes a scene in hell, is not really about hell at all. In fact, it contains no new information about hell that is not affirmed in other Scriptures. Jesus did not have to defend hell; His audience assumed its existence. Jesus wasn't trying to describe hell. He was describing the kind of people who go there: people who love things more than they love people and who have a low view of Scripture. Their character is diametrically opposed to that of our seeking, saving heavenly Father. The panned-out view of this passage fits with Luke's overall theme of Christ reaching out to the weak and marginalized. The meaning in this case isn't found in the minutiae, but in the macro.

Imagine you are in the Louvre in Paris. You have full access all by your-self to study the *Mona Lisa*. You stand 25 feet away and realize you don't really understand the painting. So, you move closer, and with every step you appreciate it more. Then, you move your eyes so near the canvas that you can see the brushstrokes. You can smell the dust. You find this close perspec-tive interesting, but you realize there is a limitation to this view as well. You are *too* close.

Similarly, there are two temptations when it comes to interpreting a text: to stand so far away from the text that we don't understand it, and to get so close that we miss the big picture. Both perspectives have their places, but they should be held in dynamic tension. The process of interpretation involves zooming in to the micro level of the text to understand word usage and syntax, but also panning out to the surrounding context to see how God uses it to communicate His truth. Both the micro and the macro views are essential to determining meaning.

The interpretive process is the exegetical process in sermon develop-ment. At this stage, we read over the text many times before using all the exegetical tools we have to discover its meaning. Once we know what the text says, we formulate a plan for how to deliver it.

Communication

Now that we know what the text says, we must answer the question, "How do we say it?" Now is when we work out by preaching what has been worked into us by study. Communication of Scripture's truth refers partially to the delivery, but more importantly to the process of composing a sermon that best presents the text.

Here lies another temptation. Once the exegetical work is complete and we know what the text means, the temptation is to present the mean-ing of the text in any homiletic form we like. It is important to remember, however, that the shape of the sermon is not arbitrary. *Ideally, a text-driven sermon's shape is based on the substance, structure, and spirit of the text.*

Substance

The substance of a text is its meaning. Because our first step in preparing a text-driven sermon was the interpretation of the text, we should have arrived at an exegetical idea—a summary of the text in one sentence. Just as the process of interpretation yields the meaning of the text, the process of communication yields a main idea—the point of the sermon in one sentence. The main idea of the sermon is the long story short.

Let's look at an example of how not to do this: the sermon I (Steven) heard on tithing from John 3:16. The point of the sermon was that God so loved the world that He gave, so we too must dig deep and give. After all, wasn't the point of the text giving—and giving generously? Surely it applies to financials! God gave, so we should give too.

God certainly did give, and we are supposed to give as well. Both of those principles are in fact true. The problem with that sermon wasn't what was said, but what was not said. Since we have but a limited time behind the pulpit, everything we say is to the exclusion of something else. The issue was not that John 3:16 is irrelevant to giving. The problem is that the preacher overlooked the richness of Christ's atonement for our sins for the sake of a strained application. Preaching that makes "points" from a text but avoids the meaning of the text makes our people vulnerable to believing heresy.

By preaching on financial giving from John 3:16, the preacher missed a prime opportunity to communicate the incredible grace of God to us in the atoning work of Christ. Sitting under such preaching, people may never grow to maturity in their understanding of the faith and thus may become vulnerable to the enemy's attacks, to spiritual slippage, to taking the things of God for granted. This is the real problem.

Failing to communicate the meaning of the text is not lying to people, but it prepares our people to accept lies as truths. With sermons like these, people can sit under our preaching for years and not know basic Bible doctrine because we have reduced difficult, rich, and meaningful texts to a compilation of practical points for living. Our sheep become vulnerable because they do not know the Word. They sit under preachers who extract things from a text and call it exposition, but never deal with the text in context. Such preachers are not false prophets, but they are negligent shepherds.

I do not believe such preachers intend to mislead anybody, but they overlook the most important part of our job, which is to articulate the Word for the people. To do this, we need to be sure the meaning we deliver reflects not just the substance of the text, but the structure and spirit of the text as well. *A text without a context is a pretext for a proof text.* By stripping passages from their original context, preachers can manipulate texts to prove any idea they desire.

Structure

The way a text is structured influences its meaning. God could have told us to have faith in Him alone for our salvation because He always keeps His covenant promises. However, instead of stating what He means in a sentence, He presents us with the stories of David, Daniel, Abraham, and others. The message is deeper because it is embedded in the form of narrative.

In the 176 verses of Psalm 119, God could have given us a list of 176 reasons why we should love the Word of God, but instead He constructed an amazing poem. That psalm is rich and nuanced, with the particulars of genre making the text come to life. To present it as flat and one-dimensional is to misrepresent the poetic way it was written.

Recognizing the structure of biblical texts has given me (Steven) more freedom in preaching than anything else I can imagine. Also, it is incredibly practical. If a text has four points, I preach a sermon with four points. When I preach a narrative that has no easily discernible points, my sermon has no points. When I preach a parable that has three scenes and a warning from Christ at the end, my sermon reflects that structure. For the rest of my life, how to structure a sermon will always be a secondary question. The primary question is always, how is the text structured? By answering this question, the structure of a sermon on that text will naturally take shape. The scenes of the story become the structure of the sermon because they may communicate points themselves, or, more likely, they will lead to one major, overarching point. This approach does not abdicate creative thinking on the part of the preacher. It simply moves us out of the way so the message God intends is the message that gets spoken.

Structuring a sermon this way protects us from two extremes: (1) slavish adherence to a fixed homiletic template; and (2) a line-by-line commentary on the text. The former can misrepresent the text by forcing a human-imposed structure, and the second can misrepresent the text by ignoring its structure altogether. Both extremes don't consider that there is meaning in the structure of the text. So be liberated! Let the text breathe. You are free from having to cram it into a structure you build or fear your sermon will sound too much like someone else.

At this point it might be good to clarify exactly what is meant by the structure of the text informing the structure of the sermon. We are not trading one set of strictures for another. We are not trading in an old homiletic structure for a new one. We are not, as someone has said, "form fundamentalists." And most important, we are not suggesting the sermon can exactly mimic the text. Structuring a sermon like the paragraph unit of an epistle is natural: once you observe the verbs in the text and note the coordinating and subordinate clauses, a natural structure automatically takes shape. But lifting the structure of poetry, wisdom literature, or law and using that as the sermon structure may be challenging. What we are after is not strict imitation, but reanimation, meaning, at most the sermon will follow the exact same structure as the text; at the very least the preacher understands how the structure influences meaning and re-presents the text in a way that considers the meaning provided by the text's structure. This will inject life into our spoken words as we deliver the Lord's message.

As an aside, this approach to preaching does not limit the amount of Scripture a sermon can cover. A text-driven sermon is not bound by length of text. There are exegetical concerns (e.g., identifying the natural divisions of the text) and pastoral concerns (e.g., identifying the receptivity level of my audience to the text) that will influence how many verses to cover.

Spirit

By *spirit*, we mean the author-intended emotional design of the text (not to be mistaken for the Holy Spirit; notice the lowercase *s*). The most obvious element of a text's spirit is the genre. A poem feels different from a letter. A prophetic warning feels different from wisdom literature. So we learn something from the genre. However, genre alone does not dictate the mood of a text. Sometimes a text's mood is unexpected given the genre: the prophets warn poetically; the epistles encourage; parables edify and challenge. The genre of a passage helps us understand the tone of the text, but each genre is not limited to communicating only one particular tone. Rather, each unit of Scripture has its own mood, determined by what the Holy Spirit intended for us to hear.

For example, Paul's letter to the Galatians is filled with in-your-face warnings. The letter of 1 Thessalonians is filled with warm paternal metaphors. The parable of the sower (Matt 13:1–23) gives great hope that the kingdom will experience exponential growth. The parable of the dragnet (Matt 13:47–50) warns that those who reject the kingdom will be thrown out. In the same chapter, the moods of encouragement and warning are both present. We could go on, but the idea is clear. Some Scripture texts feel different from others. The spirit of the text, then, becomes the spirit, or emotion, of the sermon. Only when the sermon reflects the substance, structure, and spirit of the text is it text-driven or expositional.

Conclusion

We used the illustration earlier of viewing the *Mona Lisa* to describe the process of zooming in and panning out. Both are necessary to experience all the things the artist wants you to see. It's true that art can be appreciated with a limited perspective—either zooming in or panning out. However, the real art lover, who desires to understand art at both the micro and macro levels, must both zoom in and pan out to get a complete picture of the work he is studying.

This is also true of Scripture. Scripture is written by a perfect Author. It is meaningful with even a cursory reading. However, one can clarify, affirm, and sharpen its meaning with deeper, focused study. Such study uncovers facts that were apparent to first-century readers but are not immediately evident to twenty-first-century readers. As we pan out further, we discover fascinating connections between the Old and New Testaments of which the original human authors may not have been aware and that could only be orchestrated by the single, perfect Author of Scripture. With the advantage of a completed canon of Scripture, we can look at the macro view and understand what an individual text means in light of Scripture as a whole. This might seem daunting, so how do we do this?

The best approach, in a perfect world, would be to have a functioning knowledge of the entire scriptural canon *before* we approach the text. Then, when we studied an individual text, we could connect the dots and make every connection in our minds from our vast knowledge of Scripture. Moving from the macro level of Scripture to the micro level of an individual text makes the most logical sense.

Practically, however, it rarely works that way. We know very few people with an intimate, immediate knowledge of Scripture as a whole. While we want to have as much information as we can before we approach a text, especially when preaching through a book, the reality is that we don't know what questions to ask until we have studied the text closely and discovered the meaning. In reality, it makes more sense to zoom in to the individual text first and then pan out to see this individual text in light of the whole. Therefore, this is how we will approach the text:

First, we zoom in. We will try to discover the internal frame of the text and answer the questions, "How is this text structured?" and "What does it mean?"

Second, we pan out. We will try to discover how the meaning of the text is influenced by its place in the chapter, the book, and the

whole of Scripture. Then we will determine how all this information informs a sermon on the text.

So, let's get to it. How do you understand the internal frame of the text?

Discussion Questions

1. A text-driven sermon reflects the structure of the biblical text. Explain
    the difference between slavishly copying the structure of the text in a
    sermon and allowing the text's structure to inform the sermon.
2. Consider the definition given for text-driven preaching. It is "the inter-
    pretation and communication of a biblical text in a sermon that re-
    presents the substance, structure, and spirit of the text." How does the
    preacher determine the text's spirit, or the emotive design of the text?
3. What does it mean to zoom in or to pan out?
4. Why is it necessary to zoom in and pan out in the interpretive process?

Recommended Reading

Akin, Daniel L., and David L. Allen. *Text-Driven Preaching.* Nashville:
B&H Academic, 2010.

Chapell, Bryan. *Christ-Centered Preaching: Redeeming the Expository Sermon.*
2nd ed. Grand Rapids: Baker Academic, 2005.

Dever, Mark, and Greg Gilbert. *Preach: Theology Meets Practice.* Nashville,
TN: B&H, 2012.

Heisler, Greg. *Spirit-Led Preaching: The Holy Spirit's Role in Sermon
Preparation and Delivery.* Nashville: B&H Academic, 2007.

Kuruvilla, Abraham. *Privilege the Text.* Chicago: Moody, 2013.

Robinson, Haddon W. *Biblical Preaching: The Development and Delivery of
Expository Messages.* 2nd ed. Grand Rapids: Baker Academic, 2001.

Vines, Jerry, and Jim Shaddix. *Power in the Pulpit: How to Prepare and
Deliver Expository Sermons.* Chicago: Moody, 1999.

Interpretation

3 | The Frame of the Text: Understanding the Internal Structure

The summer after my junior year in high school, I (Steven) completed my first and last day of working construction. My father decided to build a detached garage beside our house, and the builders asked for my help. Looking back now, as a father of three myself, I realize the purpose of this project. My father was building a detached man cave. You've got to respect him for pulling this off. I'm still not sure how he did it.

The day I worked on the man cave, the builders were framing the structure. All around the concrete slab foundation, they laid down long boards in the shape of walls and nailed the boards together with a pneumatic gun. One at a time, we lifted the walls into place and secured them to the adjacent house. The building was now "framed."

By the end of the project, I was intimately familiar with the building because I had framed it. I could point out all the walls and why they were there. I could explain the layout of the little building because I understood its internal structure.

In the same way, each text of Scripture has an internal structure. *By "internal structure," we mean the structure of the passage that is influenced by its genre*. In this way, it is "framed" by the biblical author. Each text's structure is unique. The reason this is so important for text-driven preaching is that we allow the structure of the sermon to be influenced by the structure of the text. So before we begin discussing how to frame a sermon, we first must understand the internal frame of the text we are studying. The purpose of this chapter is to help you discover the frame of the text, diagram that text in a way that facilitates communication, and then identify the main idea of the text. So how do you determine the frame of the text? By reading and rereading it.

Read and Reread the Text

There is no substitute for reading Scripture. The following pages will encourage you to employ interpretive strategies that will enhance your understanding of it. However, those strategies should never be used as a replacement for reading Scripture. No interpretive strategy achieves what simple reading of the text does.

No commentary, no blog, no moment of inspiration, no sermon we rip off from another preacher, no illustration, no fleeting moment of passion, no force of will, no humor, no intellect or insight—nothing makes a sermon live more than a preacher who will simply read the pure Word of God with a pure heart. If we ever have been stumped by a text, most likely it is because we did not read it carefully. If we ever had anything good to say, it is because we read the text carefully. There is no way to overestimate what Scripture saturation will do for the soul, not to mention your insight into the text.[1]

So, before we begin to study the text, we read it at least 20 times from beginning to end. There is no magic to the number 20, but we have found that 20 thorough readings begin the saturation process in the mind and the heart. Former pastor of Westminster Chapel in London G. Campbell Morgan would read a book of the Bible 50 times before he lifted his pen in

---

[1] For more on the idea of saturation, see Jim Elliff's helpful post, "My Preferred Way to Read the Bible," Christian Communicators Worldwide, http://www.ccw today.org/article/my-preferred-way-to-read-the-bible/, accessed September 21, 2017.

preparation for his sermon.[2] At this point, you will begin to see things in the text you overlooked the first few times reading through. Interestingly, this thorough reading of Scripture will drive you to read the text even more. I (Robby) read the passage with a pen and highlighter in hand to identify words or phrases that catch my attention. The process of discovering the exhilarating joys of Scripture has begun.

Ensure that you are praying and meditating on what you are reading. As you get into the text, the Holy Spirit begins to work on your heart and you begin to pray, confess sin, and enjoy the presence of the Lord. Ezra "had determined in his heart to study the law of the LORD, obey it, and teach its statutes and ordinances in Israel" (Ezra 7:10). The reading will have many effects on the mind and the heart. We have found that having a journal or computer at hand to document what you are learning is essential, because the Holy Spirit speaks loudly as we deeply explore His Word.

We emphasize the reading of Scripture in a book about preaching because it is the first step in the preaching process. Even when re-preaching a text, we find it is more effective to go back and read the text than it is to go back to our sermon notes. The sermon may have gone flat, but the text is alive.

Identify the Structure of the Text

After 20 readings, you will begin seeing the structure of the text emerge. You may notice certain commands in the text, different key verbs and prepositions, an interesting sentence structure, maybe a statement followed by proofs, or a parable followed by commentary. After a thorough reading of the text, you can almost see a picture of its structure forming on the page.

Sometimes when I (Steven) go through a text, the structure is not immediately clear to me. So, I begin to wrestle with the text. I read it over and over, trying to come to an understanding of its meaning. The text does

---

[2] G. Campbell Morgan, "Fifty Times," Bible.org, https://bible.org/illustration/50-times, accessed September 21, 2017.

not give it up clearly, so I keep wrestling, turning it over in my mind. Over a period of time, the structure of the text becomes buoyant. Through the dense fog of my ignorance, I am able to see the shape, then an outline, and then the full structure becomes clear.[3] That moment of discovery is the most joyous part of the sermon preparation process. And it's addictive. Once you wrestle with texts until you understand their structure, you will desire to do it over and over again.

At this point, the structure, the substance, and the spirit of the text will emerge. The structure of the text will become the sermon outline. The substance of the text will become the content—the meat, or main idea, of the sermon. Finally, the spirit of the text will influence the spirit in which the sermon is delivered. The sermon preparation process is a thorough immersion of the preacher in Scripture. In turn, the sermon delivery process immerses the listener in Scripture.

Take a moment to realize the great joy and privilege that comes from being a preacher of God's Word. Imagine giving yourself to years, or decades, of complete and total immersion in the Word. Now imagine what it would be like to sit under this type of preaching for just as long! People will fall in love with the Word as the fire that comes from the pulpit each Sunday warms their hearts. If your heart is warmed by the fire of a man whose soul is burning for the Word, you will lose a desire for cold, shallow preaching. The Word becomes a fire in the pews. As revivalist Leonard Ravenhill repeatedly said, "You don't have to advertise a fire."[4] It advertises itself. We preachers are to read for total scriptural immersion so we can preach with total scriptural immersion and drive those who hear us to read with the same scriptural immersion we have.

So, you have read the text 20 times and you are reading for its structure. What's next? If we want to identify the structure, we are a long way down the road if we realize that the literary genre influences the shape of the text.

---

[3] At this point we are not seeking a sermon structure, just text structure.

[4] Leonard Ravenhill, Revival Series, Lecture 1, Ravenhill website, http://www.ravenhill.org/revival1.htm, accessed June 25, 2017.

Genre and the Shape of the Text[5]

A *genre* is a literary style used to communicate a point, and God chose to compose the Scriptures using a number of literary genres.

There are arguably nine discernible genres of Scripture: Old Testament narrative, law, psalms, prophecy, Wisdom literature, Gospels/Acts, parables, epistles, and Revelation (apocalyptic).[6] As daunting as this sounds, it implies some really good news: there is not an infinite number of genres. The number is limited. There is further good news: broadly speaking, all of these genres are expressions of only three basic structural forms—story, poem, and letter.[7]

Focus on this chart for a moment. While there is a lot to learn about the Bible, and treating it this way is admittedly reductionist, these categories

---

[5] The following section is adapted from Smith, *Recapturing the Voice of God*, 27–36 (see chap. 1, n. 3).

[6] There are many potential ways to categorize the genres of Scripture. For example, Thomas G. Long, in *Preaching and the Literary Forms of the Bible* (Philadelphia: Fortress, 1989), deals with five; Jeffrey D. Arthurs, *Preaching with Variety: How to Re-Create the Dynamics of Biblical Genres* (Grand Rapids: Kregel, 2007), deals with six. The list here provides some subgenres, of which there are also sub-subgenres. The purpose of this book is to demonstrate how text structure influences sermon structure. Thus, the categories are developed around these forms.

[7] Smith, *Recapturing the Voice of God*, 28.

help us understand some big-picture ways that God chose to communicate. This is amazing. No one can ever know all there is to know about Scripture, but we can become familiar with smaller sections of it slowly, as we tackle it bit by bit. Understanding how to read and preach different genres of Scripture will be instrumental in this process.[8]

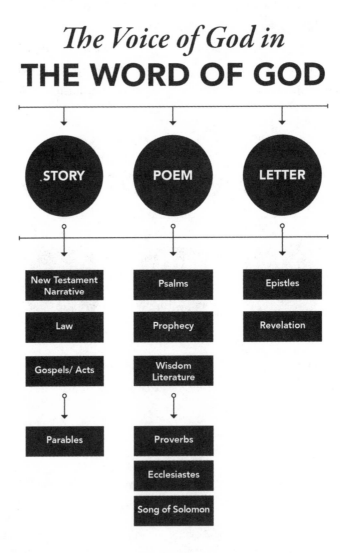

The Voice of God in
THE WORD OF GOD

STORY	POEM	LETTER
New Testament Narrative	Psalms	Epistles
Law	Prophecy	Revelation
Gospels/ Acts	Wisdom Literature	
Parables	Proverbs	
	Ecclesiastes	
	Song of Solomon	

---

[8] Ibid., 29.

There is a lot to understand about genre, but a good place to start is with the fundamental elements of the three overarching structural forms: narrative's scene structure, poetry's strophes, and the Epistles' paragraphs.[9] Corresponding to these three big-picture forms, there are least three different sermon forms we need: one that recognizes the plots of stories, one that reflects the verse of poetry, and one that can communicate with the directness of letters.

This overview is intentionally reductionist. Admittedly, preaching the poetic prophecy of Ezekiel is different from preaching the poetry of Ecclesiastes. For this reason we have noted that some genres have subgenres to denote the differences (e.g., the Gospels/Acts have the subgenre Parables; and Wisdom Literature has the subgenres Proverbs, Ecclesiastes, and Song of Solomon). They are categorized the same, but their structures vary slightly. However, understanding the structure of Hebrew poetry provides the big-picture template by which to structure sermons on both Psalms and the Prophets. Understanding narrative can help one preach both Genesis and Acts. Understanding the epistolary genre helps one preach both Titus and the seven letters of Revelation 2–3. At the same time, a macro-level understanding of genres allows the preacher to realize differences between them. In the spirit of having a starting point, we will consider the three overarching categories (story, poem, letter), then the genres (Old Testament narrative, law, psalms, Wisdom literature, prophecy, Gospels/Acts, parables, epistles, and Revelation), and then subgenres within the genres (e.g., types of psalms, sermons in Acts, types of parables, procedural texts, etc.).

A Word of Caution

Before we discuss the individual templates, we must stress that these templates are designed to facilitate study of the text's structure, not replace it.[10]

---

[9] A strophe is to poetry what a paragraph is to prose—a contained unit of thought, much like a verse in a song.

[10] When I (Steven) wrote *Recapturing the Voice of God*, a book about preaching genre, I intended to include templates to help facilitate the preaching of each genre.

Discovering a text's structure helps us find its meaning, and finding its meaning contributes to effective preaching. If you, as we discussed previously, are reading and rereading the text, you will already have an idea of its structure. You may not even need the templates. So why include them here?

We will use these templates to show the uniqueness of the individual genres. They are useful because they help us organize a sermon in a way that reflects its genre. The template is merely an organizational tool, not a rule in itself.

For example, when I physically type "Scene 1" in my study of a narrative passage, it helps me understand that everything I learn from this individual scene contributes to the larger flow of a story. As with touring the Alps, the mountains become our guide. Used correctly, knowledge of genre should facilitate your discovery of the text's structure, not replace it; it should facilitate development of your sermon's structure, not supplant it. Let's briefly discuss how genres might influence sermon structure.

With the preceding caveats addressed, here are the three most basic structures in which God has revealed His Word to us:

Narratives: built around the scenes of the story
Poetry: built upon the strophes within a pericope
Epistles: built around the clauses of a paragraph

Remember: our first task in preaching is to read the text and look for structure. Here is specifically what we are reading for:

Narratives: What are the scenes that move the story along?
Poetry: What is the strophe structure and the unique parallelism of
    this poem?
Epistles: What is the semantic structure of this paragraph?

So, as simply as we can state it, when we are preaching a narrative, we begin by reading it for its scene structure; when we are reading a poem, for its

---

In the end, I did not include them for fear that these templates would displace a deep study of Scripture.

strophe structure; and when we are reading an epistle, for the clauses of the paragraph and their semantic relationship to one another. Let's look at each of these macro-level genres individually.

The Structure of Narratives

Stories are found throughout Scripture, comprising most of the Old Testament and the first five books of the New Testament. Stories have many different elements: they at least include a setting, scenes, a plot, and character development. We will deal with the components of the story later. At this stage in the process, as we read the story over and over, we are simply trying to identify the structure.

The structure of a story is fairly simple, having a setting and scenes. After multiple careful readings, this structure should become buoyant. What may have seemed inaccessible will rise to the surface.

Moving the Story Along

One question that often comes up when preaching narratives is, "How does the preacher keep the story moving along?" If you are preaching a didactic passage from the epistles, the movement of the sermon should be clear. You may begin by stating the main point and then move along to multiple points that flow out of the main point. However, when you don't have points per se, how does the sermon have continuity?

First, remember that when we say that the structure of the sermon will come from the text, we mean just that. We are not insinuating the sermon will have no structure. Neither are we implying the sermon should ramble. Nor do we mean we are using the text to extract a theological proposition tangential to the author's intended meaning. The sermon has a structure because the text has a structure. The reason we bring this up now is because when preachers hear, "The structure of a biblical narrative should determine the structure of the sermon," they may be tempted to structure the sermon as a simple retelling of the story. This should be avoided. We are in fact retelling the story, but we are doing so to accentuate the point the author is making. Remember: the substance is influenced by the structure. So, we must know the structure well if we want to communicate the substance accurately. Biblical stories are not simply for our entertainment; they make a point. The point the author is making fits into the larger point of the book, and ultimately into the whole canon of Scripture. So when trying to understand a narrative in Scripture, we must determine how the scenes of the narrative move along the main idea the author intended to develop.

Let's take a moment and talk about the different types of narrative throughout Scripture.

Old Testament Narratives

Old Testament narratives are among the most developed stories in the Bible. Think of the long, rich histories of Abraham, Moses, and David. In these narratives, the settings will require more attention since they are richly developed. The important thing here is to spend enough time on the setting to give the story meaning, but not so much time that you take away from the main point. Succinctly and completely establish the setting. Then move along.

Gospels

The Gospel writers framed their stories in different ways than the Old Testament writers did. Gospel stories are often shorter and get to the point a bit sooner. After the frame of the narrative is identified, there will be opportunity to determine how that frame contributes to the overall goal of the book. We'll speak more on that in the next chapter.

As you read a Gospel narrative, identify its setting and the scenes of its story. Remember: all narratives don't structure their scenes the same way. There may not be three clearly discernible scenes. It's possible that you will encounter two scenes before hearing an admonition from Christ. The stories of the Gospels will toggle between the explicit teaching of Christ and the movement of the story itself. This, of course, illustrates their uniqueness. Unlike an Old Testament narrative, a Gospel narrative contains the narration of Christ included within it, which allows the main idea of the story to become clear.

Parables

Parables are another kind of narrative. They are stories in that they have settings and scenes, but they function more as narrative metaphors. They may have just one or two scenes, which is not much space for plot and character development. However, they are still stories, so we treat them as such, identifying the setting and the scenes. If the parable is too short for such treatment, then it may be collapsed into the larger context around it. In other words, sometimes we preach a parable, and other times we preach a passage with a parable in it.

The Structure of Poetry

When we think of poetry, we often think of the Psalms, for they are the most recognizable form of Hebrew poetry for Christians. However, Hebrew poetry is also represented by another major genre of Scripture: the Prophets. While these genres have different feels, the basic units of Hebrew poetry are the same in both.

It is often difficult for the Western mind to understand the flow of Hebrew poetry (for a deeper study of the Eastern mind-set, see Robby Gallaty's *The Forgotten Jesus*).[11] This is perfectly understandable because we tend to define poetry differently than did ancient Jews. What exactly is poetry? For most of us, the answer is simple: poetry is heightened language composed of words that rhyme. Hebrew poets, in contrast, did not

---

[11] Robby Gallaty, *The Forgotten Jesus* (Grand Rapids: Zondervan, 2017).

use rhyme. Rather, they used parallelism. What rhyme is to English poetry, parallelism is to Hebrew poetry. Parallelism is when an author makes a statement and then follows it up by reinforcing the idea, explaining or contrasting the idea.[12] Here are examples of each type of parallelism.

Reinforce

> Your word is a lamp for my feet
> and a light on my path. (Ps 119:105)

These two lines say essentially the same thing, the latter reinforcing the former.

Explain

> The Lord is the strength of his people;
> he is a stronghold of salvation for his anointed. (Ps 28:8)

How is the Lord the strength of His people? He is a stronghold of salvation. The psalmist repeated the idea with further explanation.

Contrast

> The wicked hope to destroy me,
> but I contemplate your decrees. (Ps 119:95)

The psalmist declares what he will do despite the enemy's plans. What he will do is contrasted with the wickedness of those against him.

---

[12] These categories vary between works on hermeneutics. We are using the categories of David Jackman and Robin Sydserff, in *Preaching and Teaching Old Testament: Narrative, Prophecy, Poetry, Wisdom* (London: The Proclamation Trust, 2008).

To structure a sermon on a psalm or prophetic book, one must identify the structure of the poem. The individual units of thought in Hebrew poetry are called *strophes*. In most Bibles, they are set off with a double space between each strophe. Once the strophes are identified, a sermon can be composed that allows the strophes of the text to dictate the movements or points of the sermon.

We say "movements" or "points" here because a psalm may be trying to make several points about a subject in a deductive manner, or it may be more inductive, leading to a culminating point. For example, Psalm 119 is more deductive, repeating approximately eight principles about the Word of God. On the other hand, Psalm 78 is more inductive, retelling the great acts of God for Israel. The psalm climaxes with God bringing His shepherd David, who ruled with a skillful hand.

To preach the poetry of Scripture, identify the strophes in the text, and build your sermon around the poem's structure. If you are itching for a 1-2-3 type of template, you may be freaking out a bit right now. Poems contain no bullet points or blanks to fill in. Remember that this is art. There may or may not be a sequential, chronological, or linear development of the idea. The poet has the liberty to take the poem in many different directions. The preacher has to work to show the unity within the sequence of strophes.

The unifying feature of the strophes is that they all are about praise. Still, the third strophe does not look like the rest. Therefore, it will receive less time in the sermon. That's just the nature of the poem.

The Structure of Epistles

Epistles are the most linear of all the genres, generally flowing in a logical sequence. Paul, Peter, James, and John had extremely urgent messages for the church. Epistles are personal letters from personal acquaintances. Their tone is one of a passionate plea to the church for conformity to the example of Christ. They disseminate urgent information succinctly. Every sentence is measured, with important theological points hanging on the tense of certain verbs. Epistles are among the pastor's most helpful tools and his go-to texts, because the essence of pastoring a New Testament church is explained within them.

Here is a good place to insert a reminder about the importance of honoring the structure of the text. The text has its own unique shape. It would be misguided to preach every passage from the Epistles as a single main idea followed by a series of sub-points. While often this is the structure of epistolary passages, it is not always the structure. Epistles contain long narratives (e.g., Gal 1:11–2:14), lists of personal greetings (e.g., Romans 16), and introductions and benedictions. However, for the most part, the Epistles are deductive. Therefore, the most logical template for preaching Epistles is to state the main idea of the sermon up front, allowing the sermon to flow from that idea.

Diagram the Text

After a thorough reading of the text, the next step is to represent it in a block diagram. For a New Testament epistle, this means you will place the text in a form that shows which clauses are coordinate and which clauses are subordinate. A block diagram is helpful for an epistle. When studying a narrative, you are trying to identify the scene structure. For a poem, you are trying to identify the structure of the strophes.

Remember: we are not imposing an outline on the text, but allowing the structure of the text to become buoyant, to come to the surface. We are simply seeing what is there. At this point, the outline may seem unbalanced and wooden. That's OK. The main point is that it is faithful to the text.

A good practice is to type the text, or cut and paste the text, into a Word document. Typing is preferred because it presents more opportunity to get the text in your mind and heart. Then, with nothing but the text in front of you, arrange the epistle in a block diagram, a narrative according to its scenes, and a poem according to its strophe structure. With longer narratives, this is not practical, since some narratives span several chapters. In that case, you must at least identify the major scenes.

At this point, we are trying to understand the internal structure of the text. We are beginning with the preaching unit and zooming in tighter to understand the meaning of the text. What is the driving verb in this epistle? Why did the author use this series of clauses? These questions are a part of understanding the micro view of the text.

Zooming in on the structure is critical because we will place everything we learned about the text into this framework. Everything we discover subsequently will be organized around this structure.

After we have read and reread the text, we begin to understand its internal structure. Now it is time to organize the text according to its internal frame. By giving the sermon samples above, we are getting ahead of ourselves, but that's OK. They simply illustrate that reading the text ultimately will yield the sermon structure. Let's talk more about how to diagram the structure of a text.

Epistles

When preaching an epistle, I (Steven) like to use a simple block diagram. Staying with the examples above, here is a block diagram of Col 1:15–18.

[15]He is

> **the image of the invisible God,**
> **the firstborn of all creation.**
>> [16]For by him all things were created,
>>> in heaven and on earth,
>>> visible and invisible,
>>>> whether thrones or dominions or rulers or authorities—all things were created
>>> through him and
>>> for him.

¹⁷And he is before all things, and in him all things hold together.
¹⁸And he is the head of the body, the church.

He is the beginning, the firstborn from the dead, that in everything he might be preeminent. (ESV)

This is not super complicated. It is just taking the coordinate and subordinate clauses and showing their relationship to one another. The coordinate clauses are justified on the left margin, and the subordinate clauses are indented under the clauses to which they are subordinate. By putting the main clauses in bold, I can see already that this sermon is going to be about Christ's relationship to the Father, to creation, and to the church. So, again jumping way ahead, just from reading and rereading the text, we have constructed a sermon outline!

I (Robby), preach a verbal outline composed of the imperatives in the text. A helpful resource that identifies the main verbs of the Greek New Testament is OpenText (you don't have to know Greek to use it). The resource can be purchased through any Bible software tech company or accessed online at opentext.org. After identifying the commands in the text, imperatives are left justified, with subordinate clauses indented beneath. Your outline moves from informative to active.

Narrative

Narrative affords a little more freedom, since we must decide whether to collapse the scenes of a story into larger scenes for preaching. Using the example from the flood narrative of Genesis 6–9, here is a basic diagram. You could have many more scenes, but this is a macro view of the text.

Scene 1: God calls Noah. (Genesis 6)
Scene 2: The Floods come. (Genesis 7)
Scene 3: God makes a covenant with Noah. (Genesis 9)

Poetry

When preaching poetry, you are reading for the strophe structure. Often this is indicated by the editors of our Bibles. The following outline from Psalm 103 is simply a re-presentation of the text's strophe structure.

> Movement 1: God benefits us, so we must praise Him. (vv. 1–5)
> Movement 2: God is merciful, so we must praise Him. (vv. 6–14)
> Movement 3: God (unlike man) is eternal in His love. (vv. 15–19)
> Movement 4: Praise God, all of His creation. (vv. 20–22)

From reading the text, we understand the internal structure, and we have presented it in the form of a textual outline. Now let's shift from the structure to the substance. Specifically, let's move from the internal structure of the text to the main idea the internal structure is supporting.

Understanding the Text's Main Idea: The Relationship between Structure and Substance [13]

It would be disingenuous to say that identifying the structure, substance, and spirit of a text in that order is inviolable, but it is at least logical, and we will make that case here.

We first discover the structure of the text because it is the conduit for, and shape of, the text's meaning. If you know the text's structure, you are a long way toward understanding its substance. God inspired His Word with meaning grander than we can imagine. Since the text's meaning, given directly by God, is influenced by the text's structure, does it not make sense

---

[13] This discussion is at least influenced by Haddon Robinson's understanding of a big idea. See Haddon W. Robinson, *Biblical Preaching: The Development and Delivery of Expository Messages*, 2nd ed. (Grand Rapids: Baker Academic, 2001), 33–50, for more discussion including exercises.

that the structure of God's Word is the preferred structure for the sermon? So we begin by reading the text to discover a structure that, once found, becomes the structure of the sermon.

Next, we look for the substance, or meaning, of the text. Since we've already examined the structure of the text, we'll have a skeleton onto which we can start to flesh out the more substantive portions of our sermon. This order is critical because we will want to demonstrate later, while we are preaching, the relationship between the substance and the structure. The sermon will subtly answer the question, how does the structure of this text support the idea of the text? Looking for structure and then substance in the text allows us to get a grasp on this dynamic relationship.

Finally, as we examine the structure and the substance of the text, the spirit of the text will emerge. There is no magic formula that will automatically make the tone of the text clear to you; but after the reading and exegetical work is done, the tone of the text should be obvious. It will emerge as naturally as tone comes across when someone is speaking. Through the work of identifying the structure and substance of a text, the third element will come to light. The structure and substance of the text are, therefore, of utmost importance.

This is an oversimplification, but this is a helpful way to think about what we are looking for when we study. We are looking for the following things:

Structure: *the way the author structures the text*
    Found by: reading and rereading
    Determines: the outline of the sermon

Substance: *the content, or meaning of the text*
    Found by: exegetical work
    Determines: the explanation of the text proper, especially the main idea of the sermon.

Spirit: *the emotional tone of the text*

Found by: reading and exegesis to open up the author-intended emotional "feel"

Determines: the tone of the sermon

Developing a Main Idea

Developing a main idea for the sermon (i.e., the communication idea) begins by determining the main idea in the text (i.e., the exegetical idea). A question you can ask to begin formulating your communicational idea is, how does the author of this passage develop the exegetical idea from the structure of the text? By answering this question, you will discover the passage's shape, which invariably will reflect the passage's genre. Generally speaking, specific genres develop ideas in predictable ways. But before we discuss genre, let us first establish some structural vocabulary. This will help us identify structures in most texts we preach.

Induction: Moving to the Idea

Narrative writers develop the ideas of their texts *inductively*. As the narrative develops, you understand what the text is about at the end of the story. If a movie or a novel is well done, you don't know the resolution until the end. Similarly, a text with a great story is not really understood until the end of the story. Since the Bible was written in a largely oral culture, truth communicated through story is an important part of the Bible's literature. Listeners were accustomed to reflecting on truth in the story after the story was told—after all of the pieces were presented for them to ponder.

Practically speaking, when we read a narrative text for sermon preparation, we consider how the story leads to a main idea. Inductive texts move *toward* an idea.

Deduction: Moving from an Idea

Contrary to the way narratives are developed, deductive texts, found often in the epistles, move *away from* an idea. The idea is so resonant and obvious in the text that no setup is required to reveal it. In a deductive text, the author may reinforce a proposition with an argument or apply a principle that has already been stated. If we are preparing a sermon that is trying to replicate the sense of a deductive text, we may state the proposition clearly up front, and then structure the rest of the sermon to follow the passage, reinforcing the proposition with support. In a way, this kind of sermon restates the main idea with each "point" it makes.

Hybrids

Sometimes a text can be a *hybrid*. It is what Haddon Robinson calls inductive/deductive.[14] In this approach, the text moves inductively toward a certain proposition and then expounds it with points, observations, applications, or principles that flow deductively from the idea. This suggests a wonderful approach to preaching some Old Testament narratives. Often in Old Testament narratives, the main point of the passage comes at the end of a buildup. Then, once the idea is stated, an application is given. Think of it as you would a campfire tale: a story is told, with built-up details and tension, the climactic moment arrives, and then a main idea follows.

We spend time discovering the text's structure so we can use it to build our sermon. If the text is inductive, we imitate this structure in our sermon by saving the full explanation of the main idea for the end. On the other hand, when we preach a deductive text, perhaps working out its idea in several supporting propositions, we can imitate this structure by stating our main point up front and moving from that idea to supporting points.

---

[14] Ibid., 115–38.

Of course, this process should never be so formulaic that we force a text to fit a mold it was not intended to fit, for example, the famous "three points and a poem" sermons we're accustomed to hearing. Rarely is a text completely inductive or deductive. As a result, our sermons rarely reflect just one approach either. We must embrace the reality that there can be hybrids. After all, there are as many sermon structures as there are texts.

The point here is that templates help us understand what *texts often do, not what they always do*. Adapt the sermon structure to fit the text. Don't adapt the text to fit a sermon structure.

From these general text shapes, let's turn our attention to genre. If we are going to shape our sermons according to Scripture, we must first understand that God chose to communicate His Word through multiple authors and through different literary genres. Genres are the preacher's friend because they help him understand the shape of the text and, in turn, the shape of his sermon.

At this point in the process, we know the structure of the text. We also should have a good idea what the text is about: the textual idea. Now we will try to craft the main idea of the text in one memorable sentence. We may need to modify this sentence after some exegetical work, but that's part of the process. It's a good discipline to construct a first draft.

We are able to articulate the main idea of the text by using the evidence in front of us to boil down the entire point of a text into one sentence. Since this can be a daunting task, let's make it as simple as possible. To develop the main idea of the text, determine the question the text is raising, and then answer that question. Another name for the main idea is the AIM (*a*uthor's *i*ntended *m*eaning).

This approach is birthed out of our theology of preaching. Our job is to facilitate the saturation of people in the Word by raising in their minds the question of the text and then answering it from the text. This is an extremely powerful teaching practice. This approach supersedes preaching to perceived needs or in response to a theological question.

While both of these other approaches may be helpful at times, we want people who sit under our preaching to know that questions the Bible raises are more important and relevant than questions we raise. It may be more work to extract the question the text is answering and then carefully examine how the text answers it. But by approaching the preaching of Scripture this way, we are placing ultimate importance on what God is saying, rather than how God can answer every one of our questions. So, develop a proposition that expresses the essence of the text in one memorable sentence.

At its first conception, this one sentence may be rough and wooden. That is fine, as long as it is accurate. You can polish it as you develop the main idea of the text. For now, we just need to get it right.

Conclusion

After reading this chapter, you may think these templates are rigid and predictable. First of all, remember that this approach is driven by our theology: if we believe God inspired the writing of the Word, that His authors divided it into certain templates, and that those templates reflect the meaning of the text, then we must allow those templates to influence our sermons.

Second, remember that the template is just that: a template. The template does not dictate how we preach; rather, it's a means of displaying the text's beauty and helping people respond in joyful obedience. The outline should not suffocate the text. Rather, it should let the text breathe. To say it another way, there are different ways we can approach the text while being faithful to re-present its structure. However, these ways are not unlimited.

Because the purpose of the templates is to let the text breathe, we do not conform the text to fit into the template. We adapt the template to the text. The template is simply a starter to help get you going. Use the templates cautiously and then adapt them to your specific preaching situation.

Third, remember that we simply need a place to start. As with this entire book, this chapter is a primer for those who want to learn how to re-present

Scripture. For those who have already started preaching but want to develop a method that is more consistent with what you believe about preaching, you may find this approach a little awkward. I (Robby) remember the pain when a golf coach tried to fix my swing (both of us can attest to this). The problem was not that I hadn't golfed before. My problem was that I had done it too long without understanding the mechanics of the swing. Relearning was unpleasant at times. Interestingly, once you learn the fundamentals of a golf, baseball, or tennis swing, you can adapt it to the situation in which you find yourself. So, whether you are just starting out or you are relearning your craft, we want to repeat that the templates provided here are not strict. You will need to adapt them to your style. But don't use that as an excuse not to learn the fundamentals. We all need a foundation to build upon.

Finally, and most importantly, remember that *we are reading to understand the internal structure of the text*. This internal structure will become the sermon structure. Therefore, if we miss the structure now, we will misrepresent the structure when we preach.

Discussion Questions

1. Generally speaking, when handling a narrative text, should the preacher work from a point (deductive approach) or work to a point (inductive approach)?

2. Generally speaking, when handling an epistle, should the preacher work from a point (deductive approach) or work to a point (inductive approach)?

3. Define *strophe*. How does the strophic structure in poetry impact the way an expositor preaches Wisdom literature?

4. What is the primary motivation for understanding the structure of a text?

5. How does the preacher let the text breathe? Should the questions raised in the sermon stem from the mind of the preacher or the biblical text? Why is text-driven preaching elevated above therapeutic preaching and doctrinal preaching?

Recommended Reading

Arthurs, Jeffrey D. *Preaching with Variety: How to Re-Create the Dynamics of Biblical Genres.* Grand Rapids: Kregel, 2007.

Davis, D. R. *The Word Became Fresh: How to Preach from Old Testament Narrative Texts.* Dublin: Mentor, 2006.

Matthewson, Steven. *The Art of Preaching Old Testament Narrative.* Grand Rapids: Baker Academic, 2002.

Shaddix, Jim, and Jerry Vines. *Power in the Pulpit.* Chicago: Moody, 2017.

Smith, Steven W. *Recapturing the Voice of God: Shaping Sermons Like Scripture.* Nashville: B&H Academic, 2015.

4 | Exegesis of the Text

Of Preachers, Preaching, and the Secret of Passion in the Pulpit

I (Steven) think I've listened to around 5,000 sermons in my life.

Some preachers are dependable, perhaps too dependable. Like geysers, they go off faithfully, saying just the right things at just the right moments. They are exact, precise. However, at times their sermons blur the line between dependability and predictability. A tinge of guilt bubbles up in listeners who nod off during preaching by a guy so trustworthy.

Other preachers are the opposite of predictable. They are volcanoes. They spew uncontrollably. They're fun to listen to initially, but after a few eruptions, they rarely emit anything new. The geyser is emotionally boring, while the volcano is intellectually boring. One whets only the mind and the other only the heart. But it can get worse.

Some preachers are slow-moving streams. They trickle along. They are faithful but may struggle with being deep and strong.

And then some preachers are rivers. They flow loudly; they rush; they roar, steady and consistent. And the undercurrent of their thinking seems to get stronger over time. These rivers wash their listeners faithfully with powerful, deep, and inviting streams of words that flow from Scripture.

Some are good preachers naturally, but they are fish of a different color. Most of us are "streams" trying to become "rivers," and as such we have to find a way to become consistent, passionate preachers, even if that is not our nature. *So where does passion in preaching come from?*

There is a false dichotomy that suggests all exegetical preaching is boring and all topical preaching is relevant. Admittedly, some expositional preaching is boring—but so is some topical preaching. Still, those of us committed to text-driven preaching need to own the critique that sometimes we attempt to justify boring preaching as "academic exposition."

But exposition—*true* exposition—cannot be boring. If we are opening the text, highlighting the deposit of truth embedded there, and proclaiming the very Word of God, the only way it could be boring is if we distort it to be so. As stated earlier, God is not boring. When He speaks, it is not uninteresting and inapplicable. That is the fault of the preacher.

God always communicates. We often miscommunicate.

Boredom is not the result of a commitment to exposition. Boredom can result from a flat examination of Scripture delivered as a lecture or a feel-good talk that is intellectually drab. Either way, boring preaching misrepresents the text.

Faithful study is the remedy for passionless preaching. It may hardly be believable that the exegetical grunt work of text-driven preaching is the birthplace of passion, but it's no less true. This is the work done in secret. No one knows what you are doing holed up in your study, but this work in the secret place tips the scales from boring to dynamic preaching. Preaching is not easy, but if you commit yourself to faithful exegesis of the text, something transformative happens: The text begins to worm its way into the crevasses of your heart. Like steely tentacles, the words of the Word writhe in your soul until something happens. A flicker of light grows to a flame, and you are enabled to understand what God is saying. The flame becomes white-hot. You find yourself caught up in tears, broken over sin. Like Isaiah in the throne room, you have heard God speak, and you are ruined. You feel unworthy.

This process—call it Bible study; call it exegesis; call it whatever you'd like—this wonderfully arduous process of learning what the text means is the antidote for passionless preaching. Why? Because arduous study of the Word marinates our passions, yielding the glorious joy of discovering God's truth. We drown our inhibitions in the Word through the week, so that when it comes time to preach, we experience freedom.

Preaching is simple: it works out of you what God has worked in you. Conversely, when study is given short shrift in the name of expediency, the heart's fire is extinguished. A sermon quickly scribbled from a cursory reading of the text or borrowed from another source likely will yield minimal spiritual fruit. When Sunday morning comes, the preacher stands naked—Bible in hand, but unclothed with the Spirit. Let's be clear: abbreviated time in the study extinguishes the flame of passion in the pulpit.

The secret to exciting preaching is not to become an exciting person, but rather the weekly discipline of discovering God's Word. When we understand just how exciting the Word of God is, we can communicate what we have learned, no matter how complex it is, with simplicity. We do not need to get amped up to find our passion because we are borrowing our passion from the text.

Of course, we don't stop at exegetical Bible study. Doing so would produce a passionate preacher who had not thought about *how* to work out what God had worked in. We have to season the Word with good communication. There is not enough fire of passion to make a sermon palatable that is not also seasoned with thoughtful communication.

We will discuss how to turn a studied text into a well-communicated one in a moment, but first let's talk about exegesis. To understand the substance of the text—the message the author wants to communicate—we will move from the larger categories of genre, which we explored in the last chapter, to close study of sentences, clauses, and words. When we discovered the text's structure, we organized our thoughts per macro-level genres: epistles, narratives, and poetry. Now we have a diagram of the structure, and we will add everything we can discover about the text, with our additions organized around this structure.

When you reach the end of this chapter, you will understand how to develop an exegetical outline. An exegetical outline communicates the structure of the text, the textual idea, and everything we have learned about the text. This is not the sermon outline, but our sermon outline will borrow, or be informed by, its structure. At this point we simply want to learn everything we can about the text and organize it as best we can within the framework of the outline we've found.

New Testament Epistles[1]

When preaching a New Testament epistle, it's helpful to keep in mind that the author was trying to make a pressing point to people he loved, perhaps with limited writing supplies. So, there is a tremendous economy of words. Not one word is wasted.

Identify the Subgenre

The first question we need to answer concerns genre. We know that we are preaching an epistle, which is the macro-level genre, but now we need to know what *type* of passage within the epistle. There are five types of biblical epistle texts: hortatory, procedural, narrative, didactic, and expositional. Let's look at these in turn.

---

[1] This section is largely shaped by David Allen's unpublished notes for the course Introduction to Expository Preaching. An adaptation of his process can be found in chapter 5 of Daniel L. Akin, David L. Allen, and Ned L. Matthews, *Text Driven Preaching: God's Word at the Heart of Every Sermon* (Nashville: B&H Academic, 2010), 101–34.

HORTATORY TEXTS

A hortatory text gives a command. We see these all through the Epistles.

> "Don't submit again to a yoke of slavery." (Gal 5:1)
> "Walk by the Spirit." (Gal 5:16)
> "Stand firm." (Phil 4:1)

If the text has a command, the command drives the meaning of the text. This, for example, is what makes preaching the book of James structurally satisfying. To preach a passage in James is a joy: Find the compelling verbs and build the sermon around them. All other features of the text lead up to (inductively) or flow from (deductively) the commands. With a hortatory text, the commands will most likely be the main ideas of the passage.

NARRATIVE TEXTS

While narratives do exist in the Epistles, they are rare. As we mentioned, we find them in places such as Galatians 1–2. When narrative texts crop up, they are there to support a driving idea larger than the narrative. For example, the narrative in Galatians 1–2 flows out of 1:10, which says, "For am I now trying to persuade people, or God? Or am I striving to please people?" Paul tells the story that follows to demonstrate he is in fact trying to please God, not man. The narrative in this case works in support of a particular point. If the preacher walks through the narrative line by line, then he will need to show how it supports this one idea.

PROCEDURAL TEXTS

A procedural text is one that lays out a protocol. We find these throughout the Epistles, but especially in the Pastoral Epistles, since in them Paul explains to Timothy and Titus what to do in certain situations. These situations include the following:

How to call an overseer or elder and a deacon (1 Tim 3:1–13; Titus 1:1–9)

How to honor widows (1 Tim 5:1–16)

How to compensate elders (1 Tim 5:17)

How to deal with those who cause problems (Titus 3:1–11)

Expositional Texts

An expositional text teaches one particular truth about God. It is simple or straightforward teaching that may or may not have a command. Examples of this are the great Christological passages of the Epistles, such as Phil 2:4–11, Col 1:15–20, and Heb 1:1–4. With expositional texts, the application may be found in surrounding verses rather than the text itself and may be as simple as praising God for all He has done. These texts do not command action, but teach a particular truth.

Didactic Texts

A didactic text teaches a particular truth, as an expositional text does, but unlike its expositional cousin, it is not a truth primarily about God, nor does it have a dominant command. Some examples of didactic texts would be Phil 1:19–26, Phil 3:12–16, and Col 1:24–29. Such texts will be taught similarly to the way expositional passages are taught.

As you may be able to see, understanding the subgenre is an important step in discerning how to preach a passage. If there is a command, the passage is built around it, and it will give rise to the main idea of the passage. Further, identifying subgenre helps a preacher identify the spirit of a text, which influences the delivery of the sermon. Now that we have identified the subgenre of our passage, we must zoom in further to examine the individual sentences.

Identify Sentences

If you are reading an English Bible, the sentences of the New Testament's Greek are translated for you. However, the sentence structure of the Greek may be different from that of the English translation. So if we are to understand what the original authors intended, it is helpful for us to examine the Greek ourselves. If you do not have a background in Greek, do not fear; you can find help from a great number of resources—many of which are free.[2]

As you zoom in to the intricacies of a sentence, look at its composition. Is there one driving verb in the sentence? Is it composed of individual clauses? Is there a series of consecutive clauses? These are all clues to meaning.

Identify the Clauses and Phrases

Clauses and phrases have a relationship to the whole sentence. Think about the clauses and phrases in Col 1:15–18 and how they affect interpretation of the text.

> For everything was created *by* him . . .
> All things have been created
>> *through* him, and
>> *for* him. (v. 16)

In this example, we see that the three prepositions we emphasized give structure to the passage. What is the relationship of Christ to creation? The answer is that all things were created *by* Jesus, *through* Jesus, and *for* Jesus. I understand this from identifying the phrases in the text.

---

[2] A helpful lexical guide for preachers who do not possess an in-depth knowledge of the Greek language is Douglas S. Huffman's *The Handy Guide to New Testament Greek: Grammar, Syntax, and Diagramming* (Grand Rapids: Kregel Academic, 2012). Also, Bible software such as BibleWorks, Logos, or WORDsearch are useful.

Identify the Meaning of Individual Words

Word studies can be very helpful in understanding what a passage means. To perform an effective word study, we should use lexical aids, such as grammars, lexicons, and dictionaries to help us understand the key words in a passage. What we discover in word studies should be recorded in our exegetical outline.[3]

One word of caution here: words only mean what they mean in their context. There is a temptation, one that I (Steven) succumbed to early in my preaching ministry, to try to find the meaning of the whole passage simply in the meaning of a few key words. While sometimes the meaning of a passage is reflected in a few key words, it is the context that gives those words meaning. Therefore, it makes more sense to understand what those words mean in relationship to the words around them. As stated earlier, a text without a context is a pretext for a proof text.

Let's make this more concrete by looking at a sample of an exegetical outline from an epistle.

Example from Titus 3:9–11

Imagine you have read through Titus 3:1–11 several times. There is a clear structure emerging that flows out of Paul's command to Titus. Paul wants the congregation to be submissive and avoid fighting (vv. 1–2). Then he gives the reason to stop fighting (vv. 3–8), which is followed by instruction to Titus on what to do if the people do not follow his command on this. Finally, he deals with those who are quarrelsome (vv. 9–11). Let's take this last section for our sermon.

> But avoid foolish debates, genealogies, quarrels, and disputes about the law, because they are unprofitable and worthless. Reject a

---

[3] See D. A. Carson's *Exegetical Fallacies*, 2nd ed. (Grand Rapids: Baker, 1996), for help in protecting ourselves from common abuses of word studies.

divisive person after a first and second warning. For you know that such a person has gone astray and is sinning; he is self-condemned.

Let's do what we've discussed so far in this book.
After our repeated readings, we have developed this structure:

1. Avoid certain debates. (v. 9)

> But avoid foolish debates, genealogies, quarrels, and disputes about the law, because they are unprofitable and worthless.

2. Confront divisive people. (vv. 10–11)

> Reject a divisive person after a first and second warning.
> For you know that such a person has gone astray and is sinning; he is self-condemned.

Now let's identify some features of this text.

The genre: epistle

The subgenre: This is a procedural text, because it answers the question, what do you do when you have strife in the church over doctrine? This knowledge helps me set up my main idea. By simply looking at the structure of the text, we have arrived at its main idea.

The number of sentences: We have two sentences over the course of these verses, and each answers the question we asked in our consideration of subgenre. There is one sentence in verse 9 and another in verses 10 and 11, which gives the structure of the text clean breaks. The audience should avoid something (v. 9) and acknowledge that some people need to be confronted. It might be tempting for some to interpret verse 11 as a separate point, but what we know about this person is the reason we avoid him. This makes the "knowing" a subordinate, or dependent, idea to the command to have nothing more to do with him.

Clauses/Phrases:[4] There are two independent clauses in these two sentences, which tells us this procedural text is driven by two commands: "avoid" (v. 9), and "reject," or have nothing more to do with (v. 10). We know commands will determine the main idea of the text. So, the answer to the question, what do you do when there is strife in the church? is twofold: avoid certain things and confront certain people.

We can ascertain the question of the text and then use the text to answer it, which reveals the main idea of both the text and our sermon: When trouble arises in the church, the pastor must avoid certain controversies and confront certain people. Additionally, after studying the passage, you may notice that verse 10 is similar to Matthew 18, where Jesus also commanded a threefold confrontation. Is there a connection between these two texts? There does not seem to be a lexical connection (a connection between individual words), or a semantic connection (a connection in the structure of the passages), but there is a content connection. So at the very least Matthew 18 serves as good argumentation for the sermon.

Words: There are several words that will need to be dealt with individually: words such as "debates" and "genealogies." An average listener may need some clarification on what they mean and why they are important to the main point of this text. It will be important to mention them in one sentence or two.

When we finish all this work, we have a document that has two things: the diagram and the exegetical idea. In other words, we have the structure and the substance of our sermon. We know what the text means and we know how it is structured. Now we are in a position to understand the main idea of the text and communicate it effectively. But more personally,

---

[4] For a helpful treatment of the relationships between clauses within a Greek text, see Herb Bateman's books in the series, eBooks for Translating the New Testament. One example in this series is: Herbert Bateman IV, *Translating Jude Clause by Clause: An Exegetical Guide* (Leesburg, IN: Cyber-Center for Biblical Studies, 2013).

all of this hard work has affected us deeply. The tentacles of Scripture have embedded deep in our subconsciousness and hearts simultaneously. Once we figure out what the text means, it will embed itself into who we are.

Narratives

Remember from the previous chapter that a narrative text is laid out by scenes. As with an epistle, the first step will be to read and reread the text until it has sunk into your heart. Then you can continue your exegetical work on it.

In a narrative we are asking the same questions we did of the epistle: What is the question the text is raising, and how does the text answer that question? An idea is going to be communicated from this text, but the way the author of a narrative arrives at the idea is very different from how, say, Paul communicated his main idea in an epistle. In an epistle, we drill down on the individual meaning of words the author used and discover three telescoping aspects of those words: how the individual words fit into the sentence, how that sentence fits into the passage, and how that passage fits into the book. However, in a narrative, we seek to understand how the author uses *scenes* to develop the idea. On one hand, it is a similar process as before in that we are zooming in from the macro level of meaning to the micro level. The differences come as we realize that meaning turns not on specific word choices, but on how the story unfolds.

Choose the Length of Text

Ultimately there is no rule about how many verses to cover per sermon when preaching narratives. The principle to bear in mind is that we include enough text to capture the whole of the narrative. This could be one part of a chapter or this could be three chapters. It could be that the narrative is told in one passage, but the resolution is not shared until later. When preaching the fall of David (2 Samuel 11–12), the narrative is about two chapters.

However, it's later in the book when you see how the implications of the story play out. These long-term effects of sin need to be at least mentioned in the sermon. In a situation like this, the text might be long, but that's OK. Although a block diagram of a long text may be impractical, as we have seen, narratives are more about the big picture and theme than about the microscopic structural details.

Identify How Each Scene Carries the Main Idea Along

Let's say, for example, that you are preaching the fall of David from 2 Samuel 11–12. You could divide the text into these macro-level scenes:

Setting   Distraction: David is not at war. (11:1)

Scene 1   Sin: David commits adultery. (11:2–5)

Scene 2   Cover: David tries to cover his sin with lying and murder. (11:6–26)

Scene 3   Confrontation: David is confronted with his sin. (12:1–14)

These are large scenes. You could break them up further, but this macro-level structure is fine and works for our example. Notice that in each scene, the theme is David's hard heart and disobedience. He disregards his duty to go to war; he is heedless of a servant who challenges his right to call for Bathsheba ("Isn't [she the] . . . wife of Uriah?"); he is unrepentant even in his audacity to commit murder, and so on. This theme of David's hard heart runs through the entire narrative. It is a thematic thread that ties all the scenes together.

This thematic unity is very important. In the preaching moment, you will want to show the unity of the story while avoiding two temptations. The first temptation is to show the unity of the story exclusively. Don't reduce the entire narrative to one proposition and give it away too early in the sermon, before a proper case can be built for it. In this scenario, the preacher offers the proposition without showing how the story develops first. The main idea may get across, but the audience does not have the advantage of learning it from Scripture, or seeing for themselves how Scripture develops ideas. They will not understand how the individual parts of a story relate to the whole story. As preachers, we want to use the story to teach theology, but not only that; we want to show how the scenes of the story relate to the overall theme of the narrative in which we find our passage. Eventually we will show how this story gets to the point of the book, and how the book gets to the point of the Bible. This is the ultimate goal, and each individual sermon contributes to that goal. We are going to look at the individual scenes of the story and demonstrate how they point to the whole of the story.

The second temptation is to engage the story line without demonstrating the theme that emerges from it. In this scenario, the preacher properly relates the narrative, but he does not show how the individual scenes of the story point to a central theme. This is equally shortsighted. We do not want to merely entertain people with a story. These stories are not for our entertainment; neither are they fairy tales. They are historical events that exist to expose the truth of Scripture in the listener's mind.

Identify Key Phrases and Words that Need More Study

If you are dealing with a long narrative, the question becomes, just how much of the text do you actually discuss? After all, a longer narrative may include several chapters of Scripture.

We should try to highlight as much information from each scene as is necessary to carry the story along. Think of the long narrative as a mountain range you see from a distance. You don't know everything about the mountain range. However, you can see the tops of the peaks. In other words, you don't see the whole range. You can't see anything below the peaks. You may not know the whole mountain; you just know that there is unity.

The sermon is to the narrative text what the vista is to the mountain. We do not have time to detail everything about each scene, but we do want to show how the individual scenes create a unity and theme. We should read from the pulpit enough of the scene to move the story along and communicate the idea of the text meaningfully.

Let's return to our example from 2 Samuel 11–12.

Setting	Distraction: David is not at war. (11:1)
Scene 1	Sin: David commits adultery. (11:2–5)
Scene 2	Cover: David attempts to cover his sin. (11:6–27)
Scene 3	Confrontation: David is confronted with his sin. (12:1–15)

These sections include all the major points in the narrative: the fact that David is not at war and an explanation of why the kings would go to war in the spring; the act of adultery; David's being questioned by the servant; his taking advantage of Bathsheba; the stark and solemn message that she was pregnant; the dramatic juxtaposition of a faithful soldier and a faithless king; David's repentance and eventual restoration. The writer of the story shows the depth of David's depravity, how much risk he was willing to take to satisfy his lust regardless of the consequences, and his remarkable act of contrition and reconciliation. We must re-create that as fully as possible in the span of one sermon.

Since there are many rich turns in this story, the preacher will be forced to make some difficult choices as to what to leave in and what to cut out. The criterion is this: each detail we share must effectively carry the main idea to completion. In this way, you are recapturing the thought flow of the author as you tell this story.

At this point in your preparation of a narrative, your outline should include the following:

- the structure of the narrative, divided into scenes
- under each scene, any information that carries the narrative along
- notes of character development and the peaks of the plot line

Once this work has been done, you will have places to hang all you find in the scene structure.

Poetry

When looking at poetry, we are not reading for a linear argument, as with an epistle, nor are we reading for the climax of a story, as in a narrative. Those looking for a grand, climactic finish may find themselves frustrated because preparing a sermon on a poem can take any number of paths. None of Scripture's rhetoric purely works off a template. Each Scripture is unique in its structure, and poetry will seem the least structured of all genres. After all, it's poetry, and as art, it is bent toward evoking feeling more than conforming to a specific structure.

We will want to begin with the same strategy of reading the text as many times as possible to let the structure emerge in our minds. Remember that the structure we are generally looking for in poetry is *parallelism*. Parallelism is a literary technique in which a statement is reinforced, explained, or contrasted in the subsequent line.

Reinforce

> *Your word is a lamp for my feet*
> *and a light on my path.* (Ps 119:105)

These two lines say essentially the same thing, the latter reinforcing the former.

Explain

> *The Lord is the strength of his people;*
> *he is a stronghold of salvation for his anointed.* (Ps 28:8)

How is the Lord the strength of His people? More specifically, he is a stronghold of salvation, or, a saving refuge. The psalmist repeated the idea with further explanation.

Contrast

> *The wicked hope to destroy me,*
> *but I contemplate your decrees.* (Ps 119:95)

The first line presents a proposition, and the second line has meaning when contrasted with the first.[5]

We are advantaged in that poetry naturally divides itself into stanzas or strophes. If, for example, you are preaching Psalm 51, the parallel passage to 2 Chronicles 11–12, you have five strophes arranged in a somewhat chronological order. But in this example, the ordering is uncharacteristic of many psalms, for it moves linearly from recognition of sin to restoration.

When reading poetry, remember that we are reading the work of an impressionist, not a sketch artist. The intent of poetry is to evoke a feeling. These words are emotional by design. So, the structure of a sermon can borrow the same emotive design. When preaching most psalms and proverbs, the preacher may opt for a thematic development. A thematic development is good when the text does not have an obvious structural unity to it.

The difference between a thematic/textual sermon and a purely topical sermon is that we are not simply discussing a topic; our goal as text-driven preachers is always, *always* the faithful treatment of the Word of God. It should be our goal to expose whatever theme this particular text contains, in the way the text itself presents it. We are looking at the theme in its immediate context and then panning out to understand how this theme is influenced by the rest of the book, and eventually the rest of the canon of Scripture. For example, let's look at Ps 119:33–36:

> Teach me, LORD, the meaning of your statutes,
> and I will always keep them.
> Help me understand your instruction,
> and I will obey it

---

[5] These examples are from Smith, *Recapturing the Voice of God* (see chap. 1, n. 3).

and follow it with all my heart.
Help me stay on the path of your commands,
for I take pleasure in it.
Turn my heart to your decrees
and not to dishonest profit.

This psalm is about the effect of God's Word, and the particular verses chosen for this sermon are a prayer. The psalmist is asking for four things. He wants:

instruction that effects faithfulness (v. 33)
understanding that effects wholehearted devotion (v. 34)
leadership that effects joy (v. 35)
an inclined heart that effects contentment (v. 36)

This is the structure of the text. The parts are each somewhat independent thoughts, unified by the fact that they are all parts of a prayer praising the effect the Word of God has on the psalmist. Once this structure has been established, everything that needs to be discovered can be organized around this outline.

We can now insert all the information we found into this outline. Did you notice there are four words used to describe the Word in this text? Also, while delight is a big theme in Psalm 119, it seems clear in verse 35 that the psalmist's pleasure is not in the Word itself but in the path of obedience to which it leads. Further, after looking at the original Hebrew, various commentaries, and several translations, you may note that "dishonest profit" is difficult to translate. Also, I believe the idea of contentment is in play here. At this point, I am free to connect this to New Testament passages on contentment, but only *after* I have panned out from this text.

A Word on Commentaries

Commentaries are a magnificent gift to the preacher. However, wisdom dictates that we don't open them until we've made it to this point in the process;

that is, after we have examined the text for its structure and attempted to identify its main idea. If we run to the commentaries before we have thoroughly read the text, we will shortcut a wonderful part of preaching the Bible—the personal joy of discovery. The joy of discovery gives birth to passion. The more we let someone else feed us information, the less struggle there is, resulting in diminished joy in our personal discovery. And less joy in our study leads to less passion in the pulpit. So we buy and use commentaries. They are a preacher's friend, and their use is an act of humbling ourselves under the teachers God has given the church. However, commentaries do not come before careful reading and observation of the text before God, and they certainly don't replace it. Nothing can. Read the passage on your own and identify the structure on your own. Then, as you embark on your exegetical work, use the commentaries as much as needed.[6]

Conclusion

At this point in the process, you have identified the internal structure of the text, written a first draft of the textual idea, and formulated an exegetical outline of the text. It might feel as though you have invested a lot of time and yet still don't have a sermon. However, you should be encouraged. You are building a foundation that will make the sermon crafting very natural. There is always the temptation to craft a sermon about a text before we know what the text actually means. It's possible to spend our entire lives in ministry preaching sermons from texts we don't understand. It does not have to be that way. The process of understanding begins with the simple commitment to read and reread the text until it becomes clear.

This process of working the text into you will pay huge dividends later when you preach. You are not just studying. You are working the text into your heart that will be worked out in the preaching act.

---

[6] For help identifying the best commentaries on each biblical book, see David Allen's *Preaching Tools*: *An Annotated Survey of Commentaries and Preaching Resources for Every Book of the Bible* (Fort Worth: Seminary Hill Press, 2014).

We read the text and in so doing identify its structure. Then, based on this structure, we engaged in exegetical work on the individual parts of the whole. We recorded all of our exegetical work in an exegetical outline that allows us to organize everything we have done.

This leads us to frame a main idea that encapsulates the whole passage. We are exactly at the halfway point. Now that we have submerged ourselves in the text, we need to come up for air. We now go to the final step of interpretation, which is translation of the text.

Discussion Questions

1. What is the source of passion in the pulpit?
2. When preaching an epistle, what is the difference between hortatory, procedural, expositional, and didactic genre?
3. What is the proper length of a sermon text when preaching a narrative?
4. In the process of sermon preparation, when should a preacher consult a commentary?
5. When handling a narrative text, should a preacher use "points" or "themes"? Why?

Recommended Reading

Futato, Mark D. *Interpreting the Psalms: An Exegetical Handbook*. Handbooks for Old Testament Exegesis. Grand Rapids: Kregel, 2007

Kaiser, Jr., Walter C. *Preaching and Teaching from the Old Testament: A Guide for the Church*. Grand Rapids: Baker Academic, 2003.

Liefeld, Walter L. *New Testament Exposition: From Text to Sermon*. Grand Rapids: Zondervan, 1984.

Mathewson, Stephen. *The Art of Preaching the Old Testament Narrative*. Grand Rapids: Baker, 2002.

Merida, Tony. *Faithful Preaching*. Nashville: B&H, 2009.

5 | The External Frame: Understanding the Text's Place in Scripture

The rooms and walls of a house make up its internal frame. You know this from looking at its plans or by walking through it. In the same way, you know the structure of a text from reading and rereading it. Now imagine that you are standing on a hill at an elevation above the house. From this vantage point you can see that the house sits on a street in a neighborhood. Now let's pan out even further, by looking at the house on a satellite map. You now see that the house sits in a neighborhood within a sprawling city. As you continue panning out, you can notice that the particular city is in a state and the state is in a country, on a continent, which is on a planet.

We have been studying the internal frame of a text: *zooming in*. Now it is time to *pan out*—that is, to investigate how the text of your sermon sits in an external frame within a biblical cosmos:

Every text of Scripture has an immediate surrounding context.
The surrounding context is in a chapter.
The chapter is in a book.
The book is in the Old or New Testament, which is in the whole of Scripture.

Here is the bottom line: *What an individual unit of text means is influenced by how God placed it in Scripture.* It's all woven together. To get to the meaning, you have to pan out as well as zoom in. You have to understand how the external structure influences the internal structure.

We have already identified the internal structure of the text, and now we look at the external structure. This may seem counterintuitive. Why not bring all that we know in the Bible to this text as we study its internal structure? In a sense, we do this intuitively. However, it is not until we know the text deeply that we know what questions to ask about its context. In other words, knowing the internal structure helps us understand what to ask of the external structure. The exception, of course, is when you are preaching through a book and you already know the external structure of the book.

In Defense of Preaching through Books of the Bible

If we are preaching through the Bible consecutively, then we already know the external frame before we get to the individual passage. We know the purpose of the book, the chapter, and so on. Some criticize preaching through books because they say it is boring and predictable by not forcing the preacher to think through the needs of the people. But this is not a valid criticism of preaching through books per se. It is simply a criticism of bad preaching. So if that's you, own it. Don't excuse bad preaching because you are following the text. If you are preaching ineffective sermons, it's not the Bible's fault.

That being said, the advantages of helping your people understand the macro view of Scripture outweigh the temptation to be predictable. Nineteenth- and early-twentieth-century pastor and evangelist F. B. Meyer wrote about the advantages of knowing the external structure of a passage before preaching it:

> One of the greatest expositors of our time tells us that he will read
> a given book, which he has set himself to expound, some ten or
> twenty times through, that he may catch the spirit of the author

and become steeped in his ruling motive and purpose. Every book of the Bible was written to effect some purpose, and it is only by steadfast attention that the modern mind can be apprehended and possessed by that purpose.[1]

Because of how our brains work, it is best to read through the book in one sitting if at all possible. This helps us identify the structure of the book. It aids in identifying key words, phrases, and themes that recur in the author's thought. Commentaries can be beneficial in this process. Also, read as many introductions to the book as time will allow. Such introductory material will include information on how this individual book relates to the other books of the Bible.

If you have read through a book several times, you will already know quite a bit about the individual paragraph units before you come to them. A few years ago, I (Robby), led my staff to memorize the epistle of 2 Timothy as I was preaching through the book. I was able to make connections that were otherwise unapparent without committing the book to memory.

This is a big advantage to preaching sequentially through books over a lifetime. Over a lifetime of preaching through books of the Bible, you begin to understand how parts of the Bible relate to others, and to the Bible as a whole.

Authorship[2]

The biblical authors did not write in isolation. Scriptures are not fortune-cookie thoughts given without context. Even the proverbs, which often seem disconnected, have an overarching theme: obedience to each proverb is an expression of fearing God (Prov 1:7). In the same way, the entire Bible

---

[1] F. B. Meyer, *Expository Preaching Plans and Methods*, repr. (1910; n.p.: Forgotten Book, 2012).

[2] For an apologetic on the authority of Scripture, see Steven B. Cowan and Terry L. Wilder, *In Defense of the Bible: A Comprehensive Apologetic for the Authority of Scripture* (Nashville: B&H, 2013).

is one unified piece of literature. God wrote the Bible using many human authors, who, while they may not have realized it, were being used of God to compose one book that is fabulously interconnected.

What the author of a particular passage says, he says in the context of a paragraph. That paragraph is in the context of a larger unit of thought, like a chapter. That chapter is embedded in the larger context of a book. That book is embedded in the canon of Scripture, with God as the ultimate Author. This is what we call the *compositional nature of Scripture*. Scripture is one book with many authors, with their unique purposes. But since God perfectly composed the canon of Scripture, we are not only free to ask how our individual text relates to the larger Bible; we *must* understand how our individual text relates to the whole Bible if we are to arrive at an accurate interpretation of the text. This is the *canonical* context, the context within the entire canon of Scripture.

Our goal as preachers is to first understand these connections as we grow in our understanding of Scripture. Then, as we preach, we can make these connections to our audience, which also will come to understand what we have: individual passages from disparate sections of Scripture all work together to create a full picture of God's message.

So how exactly do we understand the influence of the external structure of a text on the internal structure?

The Process of Panning Out

1. Identify where the text fits in its immediate chapter.

Once we understand the internal structure of a text, we pan out to see its immediate context: the chapter of the book. Let's use the example of the parable of the lost sheep from Matt 18:12–14.

> What do you think? If someone has a hundred sheep, and one of them goes astray, won't he leave the ninety-nine on the hillside and go and search for the stray? And if he finds it, truly I tell you, he

rejoices over that sheep more than over the ninety-nine that did not go astray. In the same way, it is not the will of your Father in heaven that one of these little ones perish.

This is a remarkable parable and one that is familiar to many people who have been going to church awhile. Our first thought may be that this parable describes the way Jesus feels about lost people. He leaves those who are already "churched" and goes after those who are lost. This is, in fact, His point when He tells the parable in Luke 15:3–7, but interestingly, it is not the main point here. We can only know that through understanding the passage's context.

In the beginning of Matthew 18 the disciples approach Jesus and ask Him who the greatest is in the kingdom (v. 1). He answers by saying, "Truly I tell you, . . . unless you turn and become like children, you will never enter the kingdom of heaven. Therefore, whoever humbles himself like this child—this one is the greatest in the kingdom of heaven" (vv. 3–4).

The greatest one in the kingdom, then, is the one who comes humbly to Jesus. However, humility makes us vulnerable, so He goes on to say:

And whoever welcomes one child like this in my name welcomes me. But whoever causes one of these little ones who believe in me to fall away—it would be better for him if a heavy millstone were hung around his neck and he were drowned in the depths of the sea.

We must come humbly to Jesus, and Jesus protects humble ones from stumbling. These truths are followed by a warning about causing ourselves to stumble (vv. 7–9). Jesus then launches into the parable of the lost sheep. Note that there is no sense that the lost sheep of Matthew 18 represents the unbeliever. Interestingly, this passage is entirely about believers! What follows our text is the clincher:

If your brother sins against you, go and rebuke him in private. If he listens to you, you have won your brother. But if he won't listen, take one or two others with you, so that by the testimony of two or three witnesses every fact may be established. If he doesn't pay attention to them, tell the church. If he doesn't pay attention even to the church, let him be like a Gentile and a tax collector to you. Truly I tell you, whatever you bind on earth will have been bound in heaven, and whatever you loose on earth will have been loosed in heaven. Again, truly I tell you, if two of you on earth agree about any matter that you pray for, it will be done for you by my Father in heaven. For where two or three are gathered together in my name, I am there among them. (vv. 15–20)

While this parable is often used as a template for church discipline, the point in the immediate context is about how we relate to other believers. It is a picture of persistence in Christ: When we stray from Him, He chases us as a shepherd would a sheep. Therefore, imitating His love, we don't let someone wander off the first time he offends us; we go after him. If he offends us again, we go after him again. If he does it even again, we go after him yet again! We pursue him until he repents or proves to himself and others that he was never truly a believer to begin with. We are commanded to pursue such a person as a shepherd would a sheep. This is the connection. The admonition to go after people who have broken fellowship is modeled in the way Christ comes after us.

So, the parable of the lost sheep in Matthew 18 is about how Jesus chases us and how we should chase others. Now let's pan out further.

2. Identify where this text fits into the book.

The individual text fits into the author's purpose for the book. Knowing the author's purpose helps us identify the meaning of a text. Let's continue to use our example from Matthew 18. We understand from the chapter's context that the parable is about drawing straying believers back into the fold. But how does it relate to the book as a whole?

Gospels develop differently than Old Testament narratives. In almost every case, the point of New Testament narrative is easily discerned. For example, Matthew's purpose in writing the book of Matthew was to demonstrate that Jesus is the Jewish Messiah. We see this through the long genealogy of chapter 1 and the numerous Old Testament references scattered throughout the book. On the other hand, Luke was attempting to show how Christ relates to those who are marginalized. You see this in the many references to the poor and to Gentiles. As you try to understand the meaning of a particular text, you will notice it is influenced by the author's purpose.

You will also notice in the Gospels that the individual narratives are sequential. A notable example of this is the travel narrative of Luke, which portrays a sequence of events leading to Christ's death and resurrection in Jerusalem. Everything is pointing to this pending reality.

Notice that biblical authors shape the internal frame of each particular text in a way that contributes to the larger purposes of the book.

So when Jesus tells the story of the lost sheep in Luke, it contributes to Luke's goal of showing Jesus as a leader who goes after the small and marginalized. In Matthew, though, the story has a different purpose. Matthew was trying to show that Jesus is the Jewish Messiah. This Messiah, it was prophesied, would be a shepherd. In fact, the very first Old Testament quotation in Matthew references Jesus as a shepherd (Matt 2:6). It is a quotation from Mic 5:2. Knowing this, the little story of Jesus as a shepherd in Matthew 18 relates to a bigger theme of Jesus's reign as the Messiah.

Of course, Matthew did not explicitly state in chapter 18, "See, the mention of this contributes to my overall goal of showing that Jesus of Nazareth is the Jewish Messiah." The Gospel writers were far subtler than this, using quotations and allusions. Matthew 18 is an example of an allusion. Among quotations that point to Matthew's overall purpose are the reference to Mic 5:2 in chapter 2 and the quotation of Zech 13:7 in Matt 26:31. The degree of subtlety the writer used suggests the extent to which we should bring up the book's main idea in the sermon. Taking our cues from the writer, we are subtle when the text is subtle and explicit when it is explicit. Remember: text-driven preaching is simply allowing the text to preach.

Now let's move from the chapter-and-book level to see how this text fits into the whole of Scripture.

3. Look at where the text fits in the flow of the Bible.

After examining the surrounding chapters and the book, we must determine how our text fits into the whole of Scripture. This seems daunting, but remember that we are aided greatly by others in the body of Christ who, by writing commentaries and research tools, allow us to see the connections that are naturally in Scripture.[3]

The parable of the lost sheep in Matthew 18 is an interesting one because it is repeated in Luke 15—the exact same parable! In Luke, Jesus uses it to teach how much He loves lost people. So, while the parable is the same, the application is a little different. However, there are other references to Jesus as a shepherd in the New Testament. So let's pan out to the Gospels.

In John 10:11 Jesus said, "I am the good shepherd. The good shepherd lays down his life for the sheep." As the good shepherd, He enters by the gate (v. 2); He leads His sheep (v. 3); and the sheep know His voice (v. 4). Then Jesus made an interesting statement. He said, "All who came before me are thieves and robbers but the sheep didn't listen to them" (v. 8). Since we are developing the theme of Jesus as shepherd in the Gospels, we must figure out who these thieves and robbers are.

In John 9, Jesus healed a blind man. The Pharisees could not understand this and did not believe the miracle proved Jesus's divinity. So it seems Jesus had the Pharisees in mind when He mentioned all who went before

---

[3] One helpful work is G. K. Beale and D. A. Carson, *Commentary on the New Testament Use of the Old Testament* (Grand Rapids: Baker Academic, 2007). A research tool like this one will help you identify direct quotes, paraphrases, and allusions to Old Testament texts as you are preaching through the New Testament. There are a great number of exegetical commentaries that will help with this step in the process, but this is a helpful single volume to keep on hand.

Him. However, there is another interesting point to note: the qualities Jesus listed that make him the *Good* Shepherd contrast with another list describing bad shepherds, in Ezekiel.

Ezekiel 34 describes the "shepherds of Israel," meaning her leaders (v. 1). They were selfish (vv. 2, 18), they provided nothing (v. 8), and ultimately, they ate the sheep (v. 10)! If the Pharisees knew their Old Testaments, which they did, they would be rebuffed to find Jesus comparing them to some of the worst leaders in Israel's history. They were certainly nonplussed by what Jesus said (vv. 19ff), so perhaps they got the message.

Now we are seeing how this shepherd motif is not just an interesting connection, but fits into the whole of Scripture. But there's more. Back in Ezek 34:23, God said He would solve the problem of wicked shepherds by putting one shepherd over them: King David.

> I will establish over them one shepherd, my servant David, and he will shepherd them. He will tend them himself and will be their shepherd.

We know God gave David a covenant promise that His kingdom would be eternal (2 Sam 7:13, 16). So, David's life is not just about David, but ultimately about whom he represents: Jesus, the Davidic Messiah. Jesus, like David, was a Shepherd–Warrior King.

Do you see all these biblical connections? We could even pan out further. When it comes to the shepherding motif of Scripture, what we have mentioned here is just the tip of the iceberg. There are dozens of references to the shepherding nature of God in the Bible. However, for now it's enough to know that the Bible relates to itself. Of course, it would be easy to get bogged down in this kind of study, so it is important to always bring it back around to the point at hand: how the compositional nature of Scripture affects the individual text we are preaching.

How the theme is to be understood in its individual setting will be influenced by how it is addressed in the whole of Scripture. The goal of seeing the interconnectedness of Scripture is not to do hermeneutical gymnastics from behind the pulpit that listeners feel they could never accomplish on their own. Quite the contrary: our goal is to help them be able to read the Bible. When we interpret Scripture in light of Scripture, we are showing listeners the importance of the composite whole and how it influences the text proper.

Second, the compositional nature of Scripture affects the sermon in its delivery. If, for example, you were preaching John 10, you would certainly want to mention, even if in just a sentence or two, that Jesus had more in mind than the Pharisees. He planned to be the true Shepherd Israel never had. He would be a greater Shepherd than even David! Have all these connections been exhausted in a sermon? Of course not. Yet when they are obvious, they will need to be mentioned because doing so accomplishes the big-picture goal we have in text-driven preaching.

Finally, the compositional nature of Scripture not only affects us in a stand-alone sermon, but also helps us accomplish the greater goal of allowing our people to see the way God leads His people to be saved and Christ to be glorified. Our goal is for people who sit under our preaching and teaching for a number of years to be able to see the entire sweep of Scripture. In fact, if you were teaching new believers, you could begin there. Why not give them a macro view of Scripture? Then, when you teach on a particular text, you show them how it relates to the rest of Scripture. This is possible because the Bible not only relates to itself, but it relates to itself as one grand narrative. The Bible has a story whose ultimate end is the glorification of Christ as the Savior of God's people. Every smaller story contributes to that larger storyline.

There are many ways you could outline the drama of the Bible.[4] You could divide the Bible as a drama with four scenes, with God being the

---

[4] See Craig G. Bartholomew and Michael W. Goheen, *The Drama of Scripture: Finding Our Place in the Biblical Story,* 2nd ed. (Grand Rapids: Baker Academic, 2014); and Graeme Goldsworthy, *Preaching the Whole Bible as Christian Scripture: The Application of Biblical Theology to Expository Preaching* (Grand Rapids: Eerdmans, 2000).

agent in each scene. After all, this is His story. The following outline is one way to summarize all of Scripture; it answers the question the text seeks to answer: How does God act in the scenes of His story?

God Creates and God Destroys   Genesis 1–9
> God creates the world, man sins, and God destroys the inhabitants of the world in a flood.

God Gathers and God Scatters   Genesis 10–Malachi
> God starts over with a spiritual race, a covenant people, whom He gathers to Himself. When they rebel, He does not destroy them. Rather, they are scattered from their home although they ultimately return.

Jesus is God and Man   Matthew–Jude
> Jesus comes as the promised Messiah, as both God and man. He dies, rises again, and brings the promised Holy Spirit to establish His church.

Jesus is Lion and Lamb   Revelation
> Ultimately Christ is exalted as the slain Lamb of God. He returns to take vengeance on His enemies and those of His bride, and brings a new heaven and new earth.

As we are preaching in the individual sections of the Scripture, we show how these individual pictures point to the larger scope of the whole Bible.

Forward and Backward?

Here is a question: since we read the New Testament in light of the Old Testament, is it also plausible to interpret forward from the Old Testament into the New Testament? It is clear enough that as a Jew, Matthew understood he was reflecting the Old Testament tradition of a Jewish Messiah. However, when preaching the Old Testament, is it fair to the author for the preacher to reach forward into the New Testament to note passages that may be related? To be perfectly frank, such an approach is not only acceptable; it's necessary. Remember, our position is that Scripture is one book composed by one Author. Therefore, to show how the author develops themes within the book is critical.

If we were preaching Psalm 78, for example, we would begin with these first three verses:

> My people, hear my instruction;
>> listen to the words from my mouth.
> I will declare wise sayings;
>> I will speak mysteries from the past—
> things we have heard and known
>> and that our fathers have passed down to us.

After a retelling of Israel's history, we would reach verses 70–72 and read:

> He chose David his servant
>> and took him from the sheep pens;
> he brought him from tending ewes
>> to be shepherd over his people Jacob—
>> over Israel, his inheritance.
> He shepherded them with a pure heart
>> and guided them with his skillful hands.

It would be important to point forward to Matthew's quotation of that Psalm in Matt 13:34–35, which reads:

> Jesus told the crowds all these things in parables, and he did not tell them anything without a parable, so that what was spoken through the prophet might be fulfilled:
>
>> "I will open my mouth in parables;
>> I will declare things kept secret
>> from the foundation of the world."

This connection is fascinating. Matthew says the telling of parables was evidence Jesus really was the Messiah. So, when we are preaching Psalm 78, a prophecy, we would certainly want to affirm the faith of our listeners, their faith in God and in the Scripture, by showing these connections.

The Process

What an individual unit of text means is influenced by how God placed it in Scripture. It's all woven together.

This may seem overwhelming, but it doesn't have to be. We can be aided by faithful people in the body of Christ who have researched this subject. But even more than that, our joy as preachers is that we can spend the rest of our lives both zooming in and panning out! We can study the individual nuances of a text and then see how its meaning is impacted by its relationship to the whole of Scripture. This process of understanding both the internal structure and the external structure is a wonderful gift that God gives those who study His Word.

This aspect of preparation is largely for our own understanding of Scripture, which may directly or indirectly impact what we say in the delivered sermon. Usually, it would not be efficient to spend several minutes of the sermon having listeners turn to different texts of Scripture. We must balance the goal of showing the connections in the Scripture with good rhetorical flow. The goal is that under the influence of our preaching over time, people will be able to see these connections for themselves. They will understand more fully how God has chosen to reveal Himself. We want to help them see how every text of Scripture is woven into the fabric of the whole Bible.

Think of a spider's web with an inner circle, followed by a larger outer circle. The spider who is spinning this web goes back and forth between the two circles, connecting them together. This is exactly what a pastor is doing over time. He is going back and forth and connecting the two webs of internal structure and external structure.

If you are preaching through a book of the Bible, then you have already done a lot of the hard work of understanding the text from the macro view. If you are preaching through Matthew, for example, you know the author's primary purpose is to exalt Christ as the Jewish Messiah. When you get to individual passages, you will be looking for ways Matthew is pointing to his major theme.

Conclusion

When a Little League ball player steps up to the plate, there are some "swing thoughts" running through his head. Step up to the plate, knees bent, eyes on the ball. If he were to move to the major leagues, he would still have swing thoughts, but after playing ball for 20 years, they would be more intuitive and less programmed. Similarly, this process might seem wooden at first.

First you find the structure; then you find the substance; then you pan out to find how that substance is influenced by the rest of Scripture. Yet sometimes we will be deep in the exegetical process when we realize there is a connection between the text we are preaching and a theme running through Scripture. When this happens, we are reaching the joyous maturity of someone who sees Scripture as a whole. Exegetical muscles are forming. Understanding how this text relates to all other texts is less like a box that is checked off and more like a thread that runs through the preparation process. But knowing how the thread runs takes time. Until we can see biblical themes intuitively, we need to master the basic swing thoughts that will keep us focused on hitting the ball well. So, as you are preparing and working through commentaries, you will notice canonical connections. Simply make note of them as you go. Now that we understand the text from the macro level, let's zoom back in and look closer at the text itself.

Discussion Questions

1. Why is it necessary for the preacher to zoom out of the immediate context and consider the surrounding context, book context, and canonical context?

2. What is one benefit of preaching sequentially through books of the Bible?

3. Explain the relationship between the divine Author and the human authors of Scripture.

4. A fourfold outline of Scripture was given in this chapter. Can you identify the four macro sections?

5. When preaching the Old Testament, is it hermeneutically responsible for the preacher to interpret forward from the Old Testament to the New Testament?

Recommended Reading

Bartholomew, Craig B., and Michael W. Goheen. *The Drama of Scripture: Finding Our Place in the Biblical Story.* 2nd ed. Grand Rapids: Baker Academic, 2014.

Beale, G. K., and D. A. Carson. *Commentary on the New Testament Use of the Old Testament.* Grand Rapids: Baker Academic, 2007.

Corley, Bruce, Steve W. Lemke, and Grant I. Lovejoy, eds. *Biblical Hermeneutics: A Comprehensive Introduction to Interpreting Scripture.* 2nd ed. Nashville: B&H, 2002.

Dever, Mark. *The Message of the New Testament: Promises Kept.* Wheaton, IL: Crossway, 2005.

————. *The Message of the Old Testament: Promises Made*. Wheaton, IL: Crossway, 2006.

Goldsworthy, Graeme. *Preaching the Whole Bible as Christian Scripture: The Application of Biblical Theology to Expository Preaching*. Grand Rapids: Eerdmans, 2000.

Greidanus, Sidney. *Preaching Christ from the Old Testament: A Contemporary Hermeneutical Method*. Grand Rapids: Eerdmans, 2000.

Communication

6 | Translation

At this point in the sermon preparation process, we have turned an important corner. We understand what the text says; now we need to formulate how to present it. Before we communicate our interpretation of Scripture, it is helpful to translate what we have learned into modern vernacular. Translation is the act of converting the substance and the structure of the text into a well-communicated sermon.

This short chapter on translation is the hinge between *understanding* what the text says and *saying* what the text says. Think of "translation" as the act of crafting what you'll say.

Deep Preaching

There are going to be days when the sermon just feels "on." The illustrations hit just right. The applications connect perfectly. The preacher and people ebb and flow in synchronized rhythm from opening words to closing challenge.

In most preachers' experience, this is a rare occurrence. It happens, but not often. Rarely is a sermon, from start to finish, exactly what a preacher wants it to be. To make each sermon better than the last one, then, we must constantly evaluate our preaching. We need to set up a feedback loop in order to progress in our preaching.

For those committed to the inerrancy and sufficiency of Scripture, we evaluate our preaching by one criterion: faithfulness. After all, we do not invent sermons; we proclaim truth. So, we measure our effectiveness by how faithful we are to the text, which should be the one aim of preaching. By God's grace, we stand behind the pulpit free from any obligation to express our own feelings. Eternal truth is settled. We are in the business of delivering the message, not inventing it. Therefore, it is imperative that we remain faithful.

And yet, why is it that so many times our best attempt at faithfulness to Scripture falls flat? We tried to say what the Scripture said and say it the way the Scripture said it, but it just did not come across as we had hoped. We are not suggesting there is more to preaching than faithfulness; we are suggesting that we who preach must constantly reexamine what we mean by faithfulness.

Up to this point, we have emphasized saying exactly what the text says, exactly how the text says it. However, in this hinge chapter we must note that it is incorrect to define "faithful" as simply getting the text correct. If you're passionate about preaching, then that last sentence may seem disconcerting, so let us clarify. We know there is a glut of preaching today that has very little to do with a text of Scripture, which breaks our hearts. In reaction to this, it's possible to swim against the tide of shallow, light, trivial, entertaining preaching by countering it with preaching that is boring, mundane, passionless, and disengaging. Sad to say, some of us who love Scripture the most are profoundly boring.

This might be my biggest homiletic challenge. I (Steven) want to be so clear about what the text says that often I can be dry. People can be disengaged and bored. Of course, when I realize this, I justify my ineffective preaching with an internal monologue that says, "Well, at least I got the text right. Some preachers are engaging, but they never deal with the text."

A light, trivial, man-centered sermon is a mix of God's Word and man's hubris. But isn't there also hubris in preaching that is academic boredom?

We can't excuse boring sermons because we parsed our verbs correctly any more than we can excuse light, fluffy sermons because we entertained.

Scripture is not boring. Therefore, if I preach a boring sermon, then the blame is entirely on me. I imposed boredom on the text in the same way those "other" preachers imposed their own ideas on the text. The entertaining preacher excuses his sin because he made people laugh. The boring preacher excuses his sin because he made people yawn. Neither one has really preached. I know, because I have been both.

So, again, how should we evaluate our preaching?

Perhaps the best way to explain it is that good preaching properly handles the natural tension between being theologically light but entertaining and being theologically rich but boring. This is the tension in all of us—it pulls us to engage the text while engaging people. And this tension is good. In fact, this tension does not need to be suppressed; it needs to be embraced. We are called to go deep into the text, and then bring the text to the people. If our exegesis is shallow, we have nothing to give people on Sunday. If when going deep I wait too long to surface, then I give people a dry exegetical exercise that does not help them. We must know how long to spend digging into a text's meaning and how long to spend crafting how to say what it means. This tension is good, necessary, and will not go away.

We have backed into a helpful metaphor: a deep-sea diver. The treasure he wants is not buoyant. It's not even at 25 feet. If he wants the real treasure, he must sink deep. However, if he stays in the depths too long, he will not have the oxygen needed to bring the treasure to the surface. When he does surface with the treasure, he has to polish it off so people can see its beauty. This is our task. We must spend time on what the text means, what to say about what the text means, and how to say it. There are a thousand preaching rubrics available, but a helpful place to start is with three questions:

1. Did I sink?

Did I go deep enough to find the treasure?

2. Did I surface?

Did I bring the treasure to the surface with illustration, application, and the force of imagination?

3. Did I shine?

Since the truth is beautiful, did I show its beauty or lazily offer it unpolished?[1]

Some may claim there should be no "shine" to a sermon. In other words, we just sink and surface. Deliver the goods. Break the bread. We do not need to make it palatable; we simply need to make it clear. Once clarity is achieved, our work is done. There is a part of me that is sympathetic with this approach, but it is inconsistent with the preaching modeled by Christ, who always made the message accessible and compelling. It is also inconsistent with the witness of church history, in which great men of God strove to get the text right, bring it to the people, and do so in an elegant way.

So let's get to it. We are no longer exegetes; we are expositors. We know what the text says. Now we have to figure out how to say it. We are done figuring out what the text means. Now we will try to figure out how to say what it means. Before we discuss how to explain and illustrate a passage of Scripture, let's discuss how to translate the framework of the textual structure to the modern listener. This is the next step: translating the textual idea into a main idea, and translating a textual outline to a communication outline.

Translating the Main Idea of the Text into a Main Idea of the Sermon

We need to take the wooden textual idea and translate it to a communication idea. Translation is the last step of interpretation and the first step of

---

[1] Steven Smith, "Deep Preaching," Theological Matters, September 6, 2012. https://theologicalmatters.com/2012/09/06/deep-preaching/.

communication. So how does one effectively translate the main idea on an exegetical outline to the main idea of a sermon?

An effective main idea has to pass three tests. First, it has to be memorable. Every strong preacher will work on a few sentences in the sermon and try to master them—the hard-hitting sentences that listeners will take home with them. This is what good preachers do. Of those sentences, the main point is the most important sentence that needs to stick with the listener. It should have a barb that embeds in the consciousness of a listener and cannot be shaken.

Second, it has to be accurate. The main idea of the sermon should reflect the main idea of the text. After all, this is the point of preaching: to get the text right. You may experience an internal struggle between accuracy and communication. Don't choose one or the other. Embrace the tension and fight for an idea that both is exegetically tight and sticks in the imagination. However, know that being accurate is not the same as being exhaustive. You will not be able to encapsulate an entire sermon in your main idea, complete with illustrations, proofs, and cohesiveness. That is fine. You can tease out the full meaning later in the sermon. Here are some examples of main ideas.

Colossians 1:15–18
Textual Idea: Christ is supreme over all things.
Main Idea: Jesus is everything

Luke 15:1–32
Textual Idea: Christ pursues sinners as well as the self-righteous who don't think they need pursuing.
Main Idea: Jesus pursues both the unrighteous and the self-righteous.

Genesis 6–9
Textual Idea: God tells Noah to build a boat to save him from the pending wrath of God on a world that is rejecting God.
Main Idea: God has grace on those who believe they don't deserve it.

Micah 6:1–8
Textual Idea: Israel is put on trial for not responding to God.
Main Idea: God wants a heart of responsive obedience.

This would be a good place to stop and practice translating some exegetical ideas to clear, interesting, memorable statements.

Translating the Textual Divisions into Communication Divisions

If you are preaching an epistle, you probably have clearly developed points just from reading the text. Once you've extracted them from the text, they need to be translated into more communicable ideas. This will also be the case when preaching poetry. When preaching narrative, your exegetical outline may not translate as readily into a preaching outline. This tends to occur because when preaching narrative, our points come from scenes, not developed ideas in the text. You will find that preaching narrative is not completely different, though. With narrative, you may want to boil each scene down to a statement or label.

The process for developing communication divisions is similar to the process by which we develop the main idea from the textual idea. Simply take the textual divisions and translate them into clear, memorable communication divisions. Remember that our communication divisions exist to support the main idea of the sermon. If the sermon is deductive, we might want to repeat the subject of the sermon in each communication division. If it is inductive, we might want to at least hint at the main idea in each division so the divisions set up the sermon's conclusion. Either way, now is the time to remember our priority. The sermon has one main goal: to take the idea of the text and put it in the listeners' hearts. The secondary goal is to show how the text builds up this one idea. The sermon is not trying to do multiple things; it is trying to do one thing. It aims to communicate the idea of the text by showing how the structure of the text supports its message.

I (Steven) like to copy my exegetical outline (the document we've created up to this point) and paste it into another document, called a *communication outline*. I save and close out the exegetical outline. I'm glad I've done that work, but most of it will never, and should never, make it to the pulpit. It was primarily for my understanding. I will not return to it for this sermon, but I want to preserve it, for it represents a tremendous amount of work that I will have for reference the rest of my ministry.

Once I have this new communication outline, the first thing I do is translate the textual idea into a main idea. The second thing I do is translate the textual divisions—points, scenes, and so forth—into easy-to-follow communication divisions.

Now I have before me a communication outline with a provocative, compelling main idea and an equally compelling set of communication divisions. Then, I take all the exegetical work under each division and transform it into a simple explanation of the text.

Discussion Questions

1. Define the "exegetical idea" and the sermon's "main idea." What are the similarities and differences?
2. The metaphor of a deep-sea diver was given in this chapter. What do we mean by to "sink," to "surface," and to "shine"?
3. How will the textual divisions differ from the communication divisions when considering different genres of Scripture?
4. How does a textual outline differ from a communication outline?
5. According to this chapter, what might be the greatest homiletical challenge for preachers?

Recommended Reading

Lloyd-Jones, D. Martyn. *Preaching and Preachers*. Grand Rapids: Zondervan, 1971.

Merida, Tony. *Faithful Preaching*. Nashville: B&H, 2009.

Stott, John R. W. *Between Two Worlds: The Art of Preaching in the Twentieth Century*. 1st American ed. Grand Rapids: Eerdmans, 1982.

York, Herschael W., and Bert Decker. *Preaching with Bold Assurance: A Solid and Enduring Approach to Engaging Exposition*. Nashville: Broadman & Holman, 2003.

7 | Explanation

Is there real meaning in this text? Has God actually spoken in Scripture? These questions float around the academy, but they are more than academic. They frame a larger conversation in the culture about the nature of truth. While people have these questions, they probably don't ask or answer them that directly. And neither will the preacher, at least not each Sunday. Rather, we answer these questions indirectly every time we preach by the way we explain Scripture. People answer the question of truth indirectly by the way they live their lives. We answer the question of truth indirectly by the way we preach.

While the evangelical tradition is to herald the truth that is Scripture, the current trend in preaching is to engage the emotions more than, and sometimes to the exclusion of, the mind. While sermon illustrations open a window to the truth, and application gives the truth "legs," neither of those things is possible if we have not clearly explained the text.

Perhaps the current trend of engaging the emotions almost exclusively is a reaction to irrelevant, dry preaching—all information and no inspiration. The preacher walks through the text, making observations that fill everyone's 25 minutes, and gets them quickly out to lunch. But such preaching fills no one's heart. We've heard those sermons. We've *preached* some of those sermons. But if the curse of the last generation was the dry informational sermon, perhaps today the pendulum has swung too far the other way. Today we certainly have passionate sermons. They make us laugh and cry. They move us to the emotional nerve center and park there, loitering in the deepest part of the feelings. The goal of such sermons is emotional connection. "That preacher knows how I feel" would be considered a tremendous compliment in many circles today.

But remember: there are two types of boredom: emotional and intellectual. We can't put a premium on how people feel at the expense of what they think. The reason young adults often leave the church the moment they graduate from high school is that, while they have felt what we want them to feel, they have not learned to think about God and His Word and thus are unequipped to handle challenges to their worldview. We have made them feel, but we have not made them think. Ironically, we are trending toward boredom again. This time it is boredom of the mind.

The solution to this problem is not mental stimulation to the neglect of emotional stimulation, but rather a dependence on Scripture. We are text-driven preachers. We let the Word speak for itself. We can still craft compelling and attractive sermons in which we illustrate, argue, and apply truth. But all that comes after we have explained. This order is critical because it focuses attention on the only thing worthy of it. The purpose of this chapter is to help you craft the explanation of the sermon.

Crafting the Explanation

Explanation refers to the part of the sermon where we lay out what is going on in each of the textual divisions. Explanation is, specifically, the few sentences that follow the statement of a main heading in a deductive sermon or lead up to a key point in an inductive sermon.

For our purposes, explanation has three parts: *explanation* proper, where we deal with the text; *illustration*, where we further explain by giving a window into the text; and *argumentation*, where we bring in supporting ideas—often what we learned from the external structure of the text.

In the spirit of sharpening our skills, here are some principles to keep in mind when explaining a text.

Vary the Lengths of Your Explanations

The amount of explanation needed will differ from text to text. The book of James is interesting in this regard. James has very straightforward admonitions. For example, Jas 2:1–7 gives the explicit command to avoid partiality. The preacher can move easily to illustration and application because the explanation is so clear. In fact, the bulk of the text is an illustration itself. However, James uses this practical admonition as an entrée to a difficult theological passage in 2:14–25, which will require more explanation. Then he moves to another practical section on the tongue, complete with its own illustrations and applications, in 3:1–12. A sermon on Jas 2:1–7 or 3:1–12 will be heavy with illustration and application, while a sermon on Jas 2:14–26 will be heavy on explanation. However, this is demanded by the nature of the text. The variance is necessary to communicate what James is saying, the way he is saying it. We are not to make the text say something different than the author intended.

Deal with Difficulties, Questions, and Apparent Tensions

James 2:14–26 is a good example to consider, with its discussion of the relationship between faith and works. Thorough explanation of the text will protect us from glossing an important theological issue.

We can preach tough texts with confidence because of the time we spend wrestling with them in preparation. Tougher texts often produce better sermons. We preach with more confidence and clarity due to the time we've had to spend grappling with the text.

Practice "Tighter Is Better"

When explaining a text, the goal is to capture its essence succinctly. We don't want to slog the listener through an exegetical forest and expect him or her to admire the view. The truth is, if we cannot say what the text says in a few concise sentences, we probably don't understand it.

There are many things we learn in the preparation process that will never make the final cut into the sermon. We learn them because we want to know the text and let its exegetical nuances influence what we say. However, those nuances are the proverbial kitchen tools that should be left in the kitchen so others may enjoy the meal. Just how the sermon was prepared may make for good table conversation in contexts outside of the pulpit. For now, be tight. A few sentences that clearly communicate the meaning of the text are better than a few paragraphs.

Remember: This Is Your One Chance to Get the Text Right

Whatever else we do, we must get the text right. Again, we aspire to nothing less than clarity. If there is fogginess in your mind as to what the text means, its meaning will be completely unclear to the listener.

Precision is extremely important here. This is not a discussion about the weather or sports. We are explaining the very words of God to people. A few sharp and well-crafted sentences are what is necessary to get the text right. Life is short. We only have a few sermons to preach. Those sermons are composed of sentences. Every sentence counts.

Don't believe the lie that this is all academic. When we have an illustration burning in our minds, it's easy to skip the step of giving a few sentences to explain the text. But it's crucial. The text is crucial because God has revealed Himself in Christ, Christ is revealed in the Word, and so as the Holy Spirit reveals Jesus in Scripture, we are being exposed to God Himself. The text is all we have to give. It's the most important element of the sermon. God's design is for us to know Him through His Word. Nothing less. If people do not know His Word, they do not know Him. At its foundation, preaching is explaining a text of Scripture. So, while we engage the emotions and the will, let's not trade one type of boredom for another. Let's not forget the mind.

This is also why we illustrate. Explanation and illustration are forever linked because illustration is simply an extension of explanation. So let's talk about crafting illustrations.

Stage Light: Framing the Illustration

"I cannot remember the sermon, but I sure remember that story!"

This sentiment, spoken or unspoken, is more real than we want to admit. It reminds us how powerful stories are. But if someone walks away remembering an illustration instead of the truth of Scripture, this does not speak to how great stories are; rather, it reflects a weakness in our application of the stories. In other words, if stories serve to illustrate truth, they must mentally be lashed to the truth they are to communicate. A good illustration free-floating in the mind and unlinked to truth is a bad one—regardless of how emotionally compelling it may be.

A great illustration disconnected from the truth it seeks to illustrate is like a diver who returns to the surface with an empty treasure chest. He has the chest, but not the treasure. Whatever the illustration does, it must bring the treasure of Scripture to the surface.

Everything we say in a sermon is said to the exclusion of something else. What we choose to include must be absolutely the right thing to say. We must steward the few moments we have before God's people, holding God's Word. As pastors, this stewardship is part of the larger accountability to the Chief Shepherd (1 Pet 5:1–5). In the preaching moment, we don't want to do anything that will detract from the text. After all, the text is leading the people to Christ (John 5:39), and Christ is leading them to the Father (John 8:28). Therefore, we are only leading people to God insomuch as we are leading them to Scripture. Considering this heavy truth, an illustration is good only as it leads people to the text. If it takes people's minds off the text, and thus turns their hearts away from the truth of the text, then it is worthless.

Think of a musical concert. When the artist arrives onstage, the house lights dim. Our optical senses are drawn to the stage, and the sensory perception of things around us fades. All the focus is there—front and center. The preacher is to be like the house lights. We dim so the text can be bright.

Illustrations are only good if they draw attention to the truth they illustrate. We are not storytellers or entertainers. No matter how compelling, provocative, interesting, or moving the illustrations may be, if they put the mind on anything but the text, they're off the table. Any lesser luminaries that blind us from the great light of the text fight against the very purposes of preaching. In this way, sometimes the "best" illustrations can be the worst. Illustrations must draw us to the text, so in Scripture we see Christ, and in Christ we see the Father.

The best illustrations, of course, are both compelling *and* faithful to the text. They tap into human need, but they are also lashed to the truth they illustrate. *When the listener recalls them, the truths they illustrate come to mind as well.* This is what we want! We want to embed truth in the mind with an unforgettable illustration. To that end, here are some practical questions with which we preachers must wrestle.

Topic or Text?

The illustration is like a window: people look through it and see the text. Yet in another sense, it is like a mirror. It should reflect the text. In other words, the illustration must say *what the text is saying, the way the text is saying it.*

We are not illustrating topics; we are illustrating texts. The difference may seem nuanced, but it's important. Take for example Eph 2:8–9. This text is *not* about grace generally. Rather it's about *saving* grace specifically. There are large databases of illustrations listed topically; somewhere after "gluttony" and before "guilt" is the topic "grace." We understand the utility of such databases, but their design lends itself to illustrating topics rather than texts. You may end up illustrating the topic of grace, but not the truth of this specific Scripture. A general illustration of grace is not helpful unless you can massage it to fit the specific text to which you are applying it. Illustrate the text, not the topic.

As a practical side note, frequently you will find an illustration that does not fit exactly right. In that case, you either should toss it or shape it. Sometimes an average illustration becomes a great one when you mold it to fit the idea of the text. Of course, we do not manipulate the truth, but the story is a vehicle. What you highlight about it, what you emphasize, will carry the truth most effectively.

Personal or General?

THE ADVANTAGE OF PERSONAL ILLUSTRATIONS

Personal illustrations demonstrate the text's application in my life—by success or failure. If you use personal illustrations, don't always employ success stories and don't always paint yourself as a failure. There should be balance. Personal illustrations can be some of the most helpful to use. However, it may not be appropriate to include one in every sermon. Here's why.

THE DISADVANTAGE OF PERSONAL ILLUSTRATIONS

If I try to use a personal illustration in *every* sermon, I might feel forced to reach into my private life and share something unrelated to the text—just for the sake of telling a story. At times, this leads to errors in judgment. We should never use the pulpit to draw attention to ourselves (making ourselves the heroes of every story). We also don't want to exude false humility (making ourselves the brunt of every joke). If an illustration draws more attention to me than to the text, it's off the table.

People have a natural curiosity about the preacher's life. That's fine as far as it goes. However, to manipulate their curiosity for personal attention demonstrates a deep insecurity. In sum, use personal illustrations with the knowledge that pandering to people's curiosity can be self-serving.

Long or Short?

Most people can connect with one long narrative in a sermon. But only one. If I decide to tell a long illustration in the intro or conclusion, I might opt for smaller metaphors and analogies as my other illustrations. If the text itself is a narrative (i.e., a parable, Old Testament narrative, Gospel narrative, etc.), then I don't want a competing storyline. Thus, it may be wise to use protracted illustrations sparingly in sermons on narrative texts. As preachers, we must always strive for balance.

Where Do We Find Good Illustrations?

There are illustrations all around us. They are sitting there in plain clothes, waiting to be mined for our purposes. The best illustrations often are drawn from the backdrop of our collective lives—the ordinary. The preacher observes it, tells the story, and molds the story to serve the text. What we never do is manipulate the text of Scripture to fit a story. Rather, we take ordinary stories or ideas that resonate with people's minds, wills, and emotions and show how they teach a text.

This can be tricky, but if we do it well, we will hear the greatest compliment a preacher, can hear: "Now I know what that text means." When this occurs, the preacher is dimming beneath the brilliant light of Scripture. The house lights dim, and the stage is bright.

Now that we have the text explained, and amplified through illustration, we turn to defending the truth of the text through argumentation.

Argumentation

There are myriad ways to buttress your point with solid arguments. You can argue from nature, science, statistical data, everyday observations, or logic. For the preacher, all of these are options. However, what makes us different from other communicators is that we are not arguing general truths or life principles. We are not even arguing biblical truths generally. *We are arguing* the *specific truth of the biblical text we are preaching*. This is more exact than extracting truths from the Scripture generally; we are taking the argument of a specific text. We have many tools at our disposal, but for the sake of brevity, let's focus on argumentation based on Scripture.

Move Away from the Sermon Text

Remember all the time we spent discussing how the text was framed by the biblical author? Now it pays off. We should understand this text not as an isolated passage, but as part of a whole. We interpret it that way, and we must communicate it that way.

Scripture's interconnectedness is more explicit in some books than others. Think for a minute about the book of Hebrews, which is itself a sermon. And the entire sermon uses argumentation and application drawn from the Old Testament. It is a tough book to preach, primarily because of its dependence on imagery of the Old Testament temple and sacrificial system. When preaching Hebrews, you should use the Old Testament in your argumentation. The challenge is to do this without losing our audience. The listener must understand certain Old Testament backdrops in order to fully comprehend the truth of many New Testament passages.

Conversely, when preaching the Old Testament story of the Exodus, we are wise to preach Hebrews because it helps explain the New Testament meaning of Old Testament stories. Since the Bible is one book, we are wise to teach people how the Bible explains itself, no matter which covenant we are preaching from. This is what we referred to as "panning out." We are finding the meaning of the text in front of us from its external frame.

Don't Move Too Far from the Sermon Text

There is a temptation to get so thrilled about how a text fits into the Bible that we focus on that connection without adequately covering the text at hand. This is called preaching what is behind the text rather than preaching the text.[1] Don't get so excited about connections around the text that you forget to preach the text itself. We are not preaching a topic; we are preaching the text. More specifically, we are preaching the idea of the text. The relationship of the text to theology and to the rest of the Bible is important, but it is a supporting argument rather than a main point. Over time, emphasizing biblical connections at the expense of adequately mining sermon texts will deprive people of the spiritual riches in front of them.

While arguing Scripture from Scripture, we can be tempted to move away from explaining a particular text to preaching a concept in that text. This is nuanced, but it is very important. When we argue a particular text by referencing other texts, it is tempting to get off-topic.

However, we must be careful to argue from other texts only in a way that points back to the text at hand, not away from it. Argue Scripture from Scripture, but stay the course with the text you're preaching.

Don't Turn to Multiple Texts . . . Most of the Time

To stay on point, we should have listeners focus on a single text most of the time. Having them look at multiple texts during one sermon can be unwieldy and can morph into discussion of a topic instead of a text. However, we may have them look at other texts from time to time. To *never* do so is self-defeating. Sometimes the connection will be explicit and best demonstrated by having everyone turn to the Old Testament reference in question: "OK, turn in your Bible to a related passage in the Old Testament." Sometimes the connection will be more nuanced and can be interjected with a statement like, "This is a reference to the Old Testament idea of . . ." The point is to help the congregation realize Scripture relates to itself in marvelous ways, but to do so in a way that's not distracting.

---

[1] Abraham Kuruvilla, *Privilege the Text* (Chicago: Moody, 2013).

The pastoral goal we have for our listeners is to help them fall in love with the words of the Word. The Word protects from sin (Ps 119:11); sanctifies (Eph 5:26; John 15:3); and reveals Christ (Rev 1:1; John 5:39)! Scripture relates to itself absolutely all the time. It is a beautiful tapestry, and each thread is more stunning when seen considering the whole. So show them other texts, but do so only insomuch as it exposes the text in front of them.

Our goal is to relate the parts to a whole: like threads among the fabric, like a road on a map, like a leaf on a tree, like a mountain in a range, like a grain of sand on a beach, like a flower in a garden. The text we preach is absolutely ravishing. It is special and beautiful, filled with nuance, verve, and life itself! Yet when that beautiful text is shown as a part of a beautiful whole, it becomes even more beautiful. So we should focus our sermons on both the whole (the topic of the text) and the part (the text itself). We should embrace the tension and allow pastoral love for people to give us wisdom on how much other Scripture to include and when.

We don't want to preach a topic and not a text. Nor do we want to preach an individual text while veiling how it fits into the whole of Scripture. In this way, argumentation serves us. On balance, it provides a vehicle to show how the text fits into God's redemptive history and thus becomes more beautiful.

Discussion Questions

1. Explaining a text has three components. Can you name each one?
2. Four helps for crafting the explanation were given in this chapter. Can you name them?
3. When should a preacher use personal illustrations?
4. Where can you find good illustrations?
5. What is the purpose of argumentation in preaching? Does argumentation incite boredom or benefit the preacher? Why?

Recommended Reading

Broadus, John Albert. *A Treatise on the Preparation and Delivery of Sermons.* Edited by Edwin Charles Dargan. New York: A. C. Armstrong and Son, 1898.

Fenelon, Francois. *Dialogues on Eloquence.* Princeton: Princeton University Press, 1951.

McDill, Wayne. *The 12 Essential Skills for Great Preaching.* Nashville: Broadman & Holman, 1994.

Richard, Ramesh. *Preparing Expository Sermons: A Seven-Step Method for Biblical Preaching.* Rev. ed. Grand Rapids: Baker, 2001.

8 | Exhortation

The perspiration on his forehead is misleading, I thought to myself. *He is ready for this.*

He mounted the mock pulpit in our seminary classroom and delivered what was, from every available means of evaluation, a great sermon. He had a clear main idea, and he borrowed the structure of the sermon from the structure of the text. And as I (Steven) evaluated the sermon, I heard clear explanation—he understood the text and employed clear argumentation; he understood how his text fits into the larger whole of biblical theology; and he applied this text. I truly believed he knew how it intersects with life. It was all there.

Except it wasn't.

As this "A" sermon rolled out in front of me, something was seriously wrong. It was accurate, faithful, clear . . . and completely underwhelming. After having this scenario repeat itself a few times in the classroom, I finally identified the problem. The problem was sitting in my chair. The problem was that he had done exactly what he was taught. I had taught the students explanation, argumentation, and application, but not *exhortation*. The net result was accuracy without urgency. They were right; they just were not compelling.

In this chapter, we will talk about "exhortation": the application of the text to the listeners that impresses them to act on the text.

Information without exhortation is not biblical preaching. Paul exhorted with tears (Acts 20:19, 31); Peter preached in such a way that people were "pierced to their hearts" (Acts 2:37); and Jesus moved the crowds with wordplay, story, imagination, and provocative language. When Jesus preached, you were forced to decide. This is because when Jesus spoke—like every utterance of God in the Old Testament and every word of a prophet from God—it demanded a response. Every time God speaks, it demands a response. If we preach in a way that does not compel people to respond, in a way that does not communicate that God demands and expects a response, we have misrepresented Scripture. Of course we are winsome. Of course we are gracious. Of course we communicate. But there is no point in preaching merely for the joy of it. It's not about the journey; it *is* about the destination. If people do not know they have heard from God, then we have misrepresented Scripture.

The idea that one can explain, argue, and apply a text of Scripture without strong exhortation is a departure from the historical pattern of preaching.

Perhaps the most influential homiletics text of all time is book 4 of Augustine's *On Christian Doctrine*. Augustine was saved from a life in which rhetoric was a means of self-exaltation. Yet in book 4, he applied classical rhetoric to preaching. His triad is still instructive today: preaching must teach, paint, and persuade. This was borrowed directly from Cicero and was later copied by Fénelon. This idea was slightly modified by Puritan William Perkins in *The Art of Prophesying*, which advocated the Puritan plain style of preaching: text, doctrine, and uses (application). However, the sermon from beginning to end was an exhortation to conform to the Word. The Puritans preached for transformation more than for information. All this to say, the concept of exhortation has been inherent in homiletic instruction for hundreds of years. However, a subtle shift has taken place.

We have moved away from the ancient triad of teaching, painting (illustrating with attractiveness), and persuading, to a new triad of explaining, arguing, and applying. The most notable aspect of this shift is that a form of *application has replaced exhortation*. In other words, we are telling people practically what they can do, with less emphasis on the mandate to respond to God. It is possible to apply something to someone's life and not exhort him or her to do it. "Specific application" has displaced the biblical model of compulsion and challenge.

Yet there is an inextricable connection between exhortation and application. *Application expresses how to respond to the text. Exhortation compels listeners to do so*. Application tells us what to do, and exhortation tells us why to do it. A preacher can offer "specific application" without exhortation to act on what we have heard. Yet both are necessary and interrelated. If we apply without exhorting, we might give an impression that the application is merely a suggestion—take it or leave it. Without exhortation, application can descend into a stylized self-help sermon, propping people up for better living. However, if we only exhort, then people may not really be helped. If someone is in a pit, as many people are, then it does not help to simply tell them to get out. They need motivation and they need instruction. If instruction without motivation breeds apathy, motivation without instruction breeds frustration.

Application is part and parcel of exhortation. It's not that we apply the text, and then move on to exhort. Rather, it is best to think of application as subsumed in exhortation. The purpose of exhortation is to compel people to respond to God's Word. An aspect of that is to present practical ways for them to do so. We are giving listeners practical advice and, at the same time, compelling them to act on that advice.

Our theology of preaching holds that the work of the Spirit, through a clear conduit, effects change in the listener. The Spirit gives witness to Christ, who causes change. So, we who promote exposition understand it is not our words, application, or exhortation that ultimately does the work. That's the Spirit's role.

Applying with Exhortation

The application in a sermon is like the end of a spear—crucial to the success of one who wields it. Yet application alone is useless, much like a spear tip alone has little utility in battle. Despite this reality, some preachers rush to application without first developing the prerequisite components of the sermon. Perhaps this mistake is attributable to a desire for visible results in preaching. Whatever its genesis, the application-driven approach to preaching misunderstands the nature of our task.

The application-driven approach suggests that behavior change is the goal of preaching. Because of this, the preacher rushes to apply the text. This approach yields light exegesis that moves too quickly to the "bottom line" of behavior. Yet our function in preaching Scripture is not mere behavior change, but to be a conduit through which truth flows so that it pitches toward the larger goal of conforming people to the image of Christ.

We are, in fact, trying to change lives. But ultimate life change does not happen with a change in behavior. Ultimate life change comes through exposure to the living Word of God. God changes lives over time through sustained exposure to Scripture.

Granted, the desire to expose listeners to Scripture can lead to another extreme—preaching with no application. We may mistakenly think the Holy Spirit applies the text to the heart, so no application is needed. But that isn't the biblical pattern. We want to avoid being application-driven, and on the other hand, we want to avoid skipping application altogether. We want to be text-driven preachers who show how the text interfaces with life.

Here are some ways to keep our application sharp.

Be Faithful

The application point to press is the one in the text and in its immediate context. We do not read the text and then attempt to brainstorm application points. This may turn the Word into a self-help manual or God into a life-change genie. We do not dispense advice like a kind grandfather. We proclaim a truth that will set people free, a freedom that is won by exposing them to Scripture. So find the originally intended application and deal with it first.

Put the Application in Its Place

Application may come throughout the sermon, or it may all come at the end. How the text develops will determine this. Demanding that each point have a certain amount of application may force false application on more doctrinal/expositional texts. Another thought to remember is that some textual divisions may need more application than others. So, while we apply each point we make, the application of some points may be subsumed in application of other points.

Consider the genre when deciding where to place the application. When preaching an epistle, it can be helpful to place application under each point you are making. When preaching a narrative, it often makes more sense to place all the application at the end.

When we preach an epistle, if we save all the application for the end, we create distance between explanation of the text's commands and exhortation on what do about it. With epistles, there is generally application all along the way.

When we preach a narrative, on the other hand, and force ourselves to have application for every scene, we might impose an application that is not there. This is a real temptation when preaching narrative. However, you only know what to apply once the point of the text has been made. With narrative, listeners do not know the point until after the main idea is expressed toward the end of the sermon. This implies that application is best saved for the end in a narrative sermon. In this way, the narrative is both inductive and deductive—working both toward and from the main idea.

Remember the Trajectory

Application may move from the general to the specific:

For example, one could make a case for the sanctify of life from Ps 139:13–14. If we are "remarkably and wondrously made," then this general truth can be applied to the specific issue of abortion. Many texts give general principles about the character and nature of God from which we can extract practical daily applications. For another example consider the theologically loaded passage Phil 2:1–11. From the glorious theological general truth of the humiliation and exaltation of Christ, one can make many specific applications. From the general truth of Christ's humiliation, we can deduce that we should not manipulate conversations to make ourselves look better than reality.

Spirit-Driven APPLICATION

Application moves from the GENERAL to the SPECIFIC.

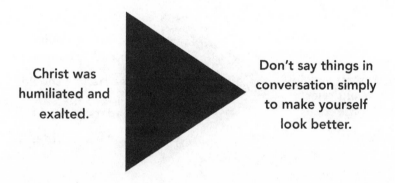

Christ was humiliated and exalted.

Don't say things in conversation simply to make yourself look better.

Application may move from the specific to the general:

From the specific admonition in Titus 3:9–11 that the pastor must avoid silly controversies and confront the sinning brother, we may conclude that God wants order in local congregations. Such a move from specific to general is helpful because it allows us to pan out from very specific issues in the text and show how they apply on a broader scale.

Spirit-Driven
APPLICATION

Application moves from the SPECIFIC to the GENERAL.

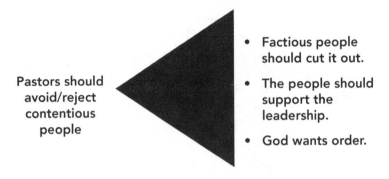

Pastors should
avoid/reject
contentious
people

- Factious people should cut it out.

- The people should support the leadership.

- God wants order.

Weave

This is the most important aspect of application, and no doubt the hardest to accomplish. What we mean by weaving is *making the illustration of the sermon and the application one unit*—weaving them together.

Imagine a sermon that begins with a compelling illustration. The preacher has us right where he wants us. Then he says, "That's just like what Paul is saying in this text . . ." or, "Now, this relates to our text in this way . . ." What the people heard was, "The story is over. Go back to sleep."

The end of the illustration is the most pivotal moment for application. In this way, the last line of the illustration should be the first line of the application. When attention is arrested with a great illustration, that is the time to strike with application. The best applications tease out an illustration. You might wonder if this is technically illustration or application. Often, that blurred line is a sign of a well-woven application.

Perhaps the balance is best expressed in Titus 1:1, where Paul described faith as "the knowledge of the truth that leads to godliness." This is not just life change. This is not just knowledge. This is what believers want: to know the Word in such a way that it changes their lives. This is the Word that cuts, then heals. Application that flows from a sermon driven by the text should never be dull because it is committed to the work of life transformation. The Word of God is alive. The Word is active. The Word is sharp.

Discussion Questions

1. Should application come at the exclusion of exhortation? Why or why not? If not, what is the connection between application and exhortation?
2. How can the preacher's desire for exegetical accuracy at times mute his prophetic voice?
3. How does a preacher put application in its correct place?
4. How does the genre of the text impact where the preacher places application in the sermon?
5. How should the preacher weave illustration and application?

Recommended Reading

Doriani, Daniel M. *Putting the Truth to Work: The Theory and Practice of Biblical Application*. Phillipsburg, NJ: Presbyterian & Reformed, 2001.

Duduit, Michael. *Handbook of Contemporary Preaching*. Nashville: Broadman Press, 1992.

Mohler, R. Albert, Jr. *He is Not Silent: Preaching in a Postmodern World*. Chicago: Moody, 2008

Robinson, Haddon W., and Craig Brian Larsen. *The Art and Craft of Biblical Preaching*. Grand Rapids: Zondervan, 2005.

Robinson, Haddon W. "The Heresy of Application: It's When We're Applying Scripture That Error Is Most Likely to Creep In." *Leadership* 18 (1997): 20–27.

9 | Conclusions

A preacher must know when the sermon is over. There should be no question that the message has reached a boil and is now complete. Sometimes we preachers do not end our sermons soon enough because we forget the purpose of the conclusion. We communicate, in essence, "Now that I have repeated all my main points, let me tell you two stories that will make this really come alive." Conversely, there is a temptation to do too little with the conclusion: "Well, I think I'm done; let's just stop there." The former approach punishes the faithful listener by giving him the same information over again. The latter approach is too abrupt.

The conclusion has two goals: reinforcement and response. We are trying to, like turning a screw once more, drive the main idea of the sermon into the hearts and minds of the listeners. We then want to let them know what they should do about it. That's it. These two goals are enough to craft a solid and simple conclusion. Let's discover what a conclusion must do and discuss potential content.

A Conclusion Must Reinforce the Main Idea

The conclusion is the last opportunity to drive home the point of the text. Like the introduction, the conclusion should faithfully represent the idea of the sermon. It should not be forced or unrelated. If it needs explanation, that is an indicator the conclusion may be a stretch.

The main idea of the sermon is the one piece of information you want listeners to grasp. If there is a story or an idea that overshadows the main idea, then we have not done justice to the text. Remember: this all flows from our theology of the Word of God. We believe God has revealed Himself in His Word, and therefore God is knowable through His Word.

A Conclusion Must Bring the Message to a Definite Stop

The challenge of a great conclusion is to say things so concisely that we both summarize the main intent of the message and leave the listener wanting more. Some preachers are good at flying, but they do not know how to land the plane. The worst possible scenario is for the listener to feel as if the sermon is about to end, but just at that glorious moment of ending, the sermon revs up again and takes another lap of repetition. The reason sermons go long is sometimes that we have a lot to say. Other times sermons go long because we have not decided where the sermon will end.

Think of it as like a road trip. Unless you are on an existential trip of self-discovery, you decide on a destination before you begin. This is the idea of the conclusion. We choose where we will end.

A Conclusion Should Be Relatively Brief

If the conclusion is done well, a few minutes are all that will be needed. For a 35-minute sermon, consider a conclusion that is around five minutes. There is room for flexibility, but this is a good guide.

A Conclusion Should Have a Simple Structure

The structure of a good conclusion should be simple. Templates are just guides. There are no exact ways to properly write a conclusion. However, let us suggest a template that will give you a starting place.

Repeat the main idea.

The conclusion can begin by repeating the main idea of the sermon, or summarizing. This is a simple sentence or two. Beware of redundancy here. You want something that will reinforce without predictability. Try to say the same thing in a different way.

Make one major move.

After reinforcing the main idea, the conclusion should make a main move and then stop. A final move in the conclusion is justified only when it moves the main idea from the general to the specific, making it clearer in a relatively short amount of time. That is quite enough.

Encourage a response.

When God speaks, a response is required. If God has revealed Himself in His Word, then we must respond. Our responsibility is to facilitate a practical way for listeners to respond. If there has been application in the sermon, now is a good time to reinforce the application and press them to respond. This is the time when you try to facilitate what the Lord may be doing in their lives. We will discuss this more in a later chapter.

So, what can you use for your one main move? There are an unlimited number of options. Here are a few:

1. Close with an illustration.
    This can be very effective. Sometimes it is effective to share a personal illustration here so the listener can see how you have processed the sermon in your life. If you opt for a personal illustration, remember that all the rules of personal illustrations apply here. As mentioned earlier, don't be the hero of every story; don't be the brunt of every joke; and don't overuse them. Predictability in conclusions may prematurely give the listener a mental clue the sermon is done. Don't always use a story. Mix it up for variety.

2. Close with a summary.

    This can be a helpful approach. Just make sure you aren't redundant. You may attempt to say the same thing, but in a slightly different way.

3. Show how this text fits into the big picture.

    Say you are preaching through a book of the Bible. It is possible that people will lose sight of how a text fits into the larger whole of Scripture. The conclusion is a great time to back out and demonstrate how the text fits into the whole of Scripture. Like any other method, this could get redundant if it is your go-to conclusion technique. However, it is helpful to show how the part fits into the whole from time to time since one of our goals is to teach people how the Bible relates to itself.

4. Deal with the last point or the entire message.

    This is a question preachers wrestle with from time to time: Should the conclusion deal with the last point or the entire message? In all honesty, this is subjective and it depends on the sermon. However, a guiding principle is to use the conclusion to drive home the *main idea* of the sermon.

    If you are preaching an inductive text, like a narrative, and all the weight of the narrative is in the last scene, including the main idea, then yes, just use the conclusion to drive home the last point since the last point contains the main idea of the sermon.

5. Bring up the application of the introduction.

    If you are preaching a difficult text, you may opt to bring up application in the introduction. As you are getting into a seemingly obscure text, you can hint as to how it will apply practically, motivating the listener to hang in there through some difficult terrain. If you use that introduction technique, then the conclusion is a great place to reinforce the application raised in the introduction.

6. Complete the storyline of the introduction.

   This is called *bookending*. You begin a story in the introduction, and then you complete it in the conclusion. This is a great technique if you don't use it too much. Overuse breeds predictability and audience boredom. Second, you have to make sure the introduction stands on its own merits. In other words, you might lose people if they spend the meat of your sermon wondering how the story in your introduction ends. Certainly you can begin a narrative in the introduction and finish it in the conclusion. However, the introductory portion of the narrative must be capable of standing alone.

A Final Note

Whether you choose to handwrite or type out sermons or not, it is advisable to always do so with the conclusion and the introduction. Having the introduction and the conclusion before you in manuscript form keeps them crisply in your mind and is the best way to enter the pulpit with confidence.

Discussion Questions

1. How long should a conclusion be?
2. Should the conclusion always end with a story?
3. Should the conclusion drive home the point of the whole sermon, or just the last point?
4. Should the conclusion include ways to respond? Why or why not?
5. Is it advisable to "bookend" the sermon by completing a story line that surfaced in the introduction?

Recommended Reading

Dabney, Robert L. *Evangelical Eloquence: A Course of Lectures on Preaching.* Edinburgh: Banner of Truth Trust, 1999.

MacArthur, John, Jr., and the Master's Seminary Faculty. *Rediscovering Expository Preaching.* Edited by Richard Mayhue. Dallas: Word, 1992.

Richard, Ramesh. *Preparing Expository Sermons: A Seven-Step Method for Biblical Preaching.* Rev. ed. Grand Rapids: Baker, 2001.

10 | Introductions

It may seem odd to place the introduction chapter at the end. However, a preacher is unable to write the introduction until the message is complete. Introductions are essential to garner the attention of your audience. It's difficult to overcome a bad introduction. It may seem unfair, but that's just the way it is. The first five minutes builds a case for the remaining 35 minutes. You may have stellar exegesis and some winning illustrations, but if your introduction is weak, the sermon probably will not recover.

We decide to shop in a certain store, pursue a certain college, or keep reading a book when we are attracted to the way it is introduced to us. This is not being shallow; this is simply the way we are designed. If something is not worth our time and investment, then we are well served to move along. Life is too short to read good books; we must read the best books. Life is too short to waste time with things that will not help us. We must pursue the best. God has placed in every individual this capacity to bypass unworthy uses of time.

Therefore, if our sermon introduction is not winsome and compelling, we can hardly blame people if they do not stick around to hear the rest of the sermon. They may not physically walk out of the sermon, but just because someone is sitting with his eyes open does not mean he is listening. Perhaps he is just polite. All this to say, the introduction sets a tone for the sermon and communicates information about the preacher delivering it.

There are two classic mistakes that render introductions ineffective.

The introduction is too long. This is subjective, of course. However, if I plan to preach 35–40 minutes and I spend 10 minutes in introduction, then I have spent over a quarter of my sermon setting up what I was trying to say instead of just saying it. For just about every "normal" sermon, a 5-minute introduction is a good goal. This will vary depending on specific preaching situations. For example, if you are a guest preacher, you may take a moment to thank the church for allowing you to come. If you are speaking to students, you may need to establish more context. However, these are exceptions and not the rule. A great introduction is a short introduction.

The introduction takes too many turns. An introduction that takes too many turns may look like this: an illustration, a joke, and then some application, along with cultural commentary. All of this may be interesting, but when you over-invest in the introduction, you are diminishing the body of the sermon. You should not back up the dump truck of information in the first five minutes. You can blow them away; just don't bury them.

Imagine you are taking listeners to a destination. If you take multiple turns that do not make sense, you can't blame them for getting out of the car. As you begin, they should see the destination clearly. If you turn (which may or may not be necessary), they should see that the destination is still in sight. If you turn again, it should only be because you want to get closer to the destination, to clarify the main idea of the sermon so they can see even more clearly where you are taking them.

Employ several well-measured sentences. Set up the text and get to it. Over time, people will take your words seriously if they know you have measured them out. A rambler rarely will be taken seriously. The introduction should make two moves, possibly three. We set up what we want to say, perhaps with an illustration or an application, and then we jump into it. That's it. The more time we spend on introduction, the less time there is for faithful exposition. So, steward the time wisely.

How do you frame a compelling introduction? You must (1) look to the main idea, (2) frame the question the text is raising, and possibly (3) raise practical application.

Look to the Main Idea

This assumes you have drafted the sermon before drafting the introduction and understand where the points are going. If the main idea is not crystal clear in your mind, then you will not be able to pinpoint it in the introduction.

Focusing on the main idea of the sermon flows from our theology of the Word. If we believe God has spoken in this passage, then from start to finish we are trying to set up what God has said. The purpose of the sermon introduction is to set up the main idea of the sermon.

Raise the Question the Main Idea Answers

A great introduction convinces the listener that the question a text raises is the most important topic in that moment. This is no small feat. Listeners have family issues and financial pressures, and may not even want to be there. You have a passage that seems obscure, obtuse, and irrelevant. *You* understand that this passage is relevant, but they might not. The sermon they hear will display the relevance of this text—and the introduction is where you set the hook, making them believe this passage is the most important thing to think about for the time being.

Again, the purpose of the introduction is to frame the question *the* text raises and show its relevance. That's it. A classic way to do this is to ask the question that the text is raising at the end of the introduction. To make this effective, we must not ask many other rhetorical questions. It throws people off and gets them distracted. If you ask a question, it should be the question the text is raising. The sermon answers the question.

What about Narratives?

With narratives, you may not need a classic introduction. You can just begin by telling the story or setting the scene. This can be an effective way to preach the text. However, let's assume you are preaching a text that is a story and you want to set it up with a formal introduction. The key is to raise the subject of the text without giving away its main idea too early.

For example, the story of the fall is about God's saving grace toward Adam despite deep failure. A good introduction would bring up the topic of failure without expounding it. The full main idea can come later in the sermon.

In this way, as you begin the narrative, you are communicating that this story is about something. As you begin the journey together, you are telling listeners what to look for in the story. This story has a bullet-like application that is intended to be clear. You know this, so you set them up to see it too. This introduction will set the stage for unity throughout the sermon.

Set Up the Question

To set up the question of the text, we begin with the end in mind. The preacher knows that at the end of this introduction, he wants one solid question embedded in the minds of his listeners. So he asks himself, *What will set up the question the text is raising?* A story? A personal anecdote? A historical example? The recitation of a certain text? You have options.

Remember that the illustration fairy is not going to drop the perfect illustration in your brain at just the right moment. It's more likely you will have an illustration that is sort of good. It's just OK. Then you will massage and adjust it, using wordplay and imagination, until that illustration sets up the text.

Here's an example. I (Steven) heard a great illustration about a large passenger jet that was stalled before takeoff because a few birds were on the runway. That's it. The whole story. No surprise ending, just birds on the runway. By itself, it is hardly a mind-blowing event. No news outlet picked the story up. However, when it was told, it was fantastic. The preacher applied it to Christians who, like the plane, have all the lift and thrust they need to take off and do great things, but they are sidelined by seemingly small, besetting sins. The preacher took a basic event and made a great introduction out of it.

Limit the Moves an Introduction Makes

A "move" is a story, an illustration, or any new thought you introduce. The bane of a good introduction is trying to do too much with it. Think of one or two moves, and then set up the application of the text.

The outline is simple:

First Move

Second Move
(if needed)

Main Idea/Subject

The image on the next page shows how you can visualize the elements of an ideal introduction.

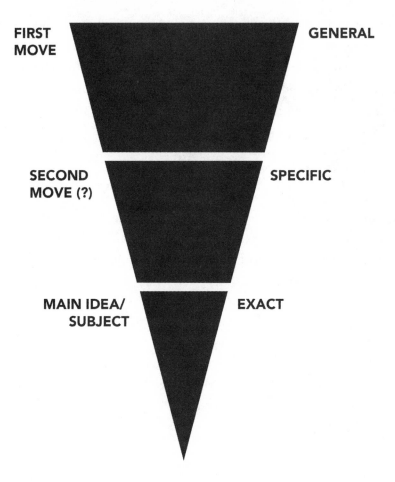

FIRST MOVE — GENERAL

SECOND MOVE (?) — SPECIFIC

MAIN IDEA/ SUBJECT — EXACT

The ideal introduction does one thing and then gets into the text. It should carry listeners along in a tide that will wash them up on the shore of the main idea. They should know exactly where the sermon is going.

Lead with Application

When we raise a potential application in the introduction, we make a contract with the listener. We promise them that Scripture speaks to this issue. To make good on that promise, we provide them the solid meat of the Word, then connect the theology with the application in the message.

This is a good option for passages that are especially theologically dense or that give the initial appearance they are disconnected from the listener's life.

The Process

So how do we craft a solid introduction? Locate the question the text is raising. This likely will be the last sentence of the introduction. Then cultivate a "move" that will get the listener to that question. Make one or two moves, state the question the text is raising, and then move on to the exposition proper. Now write out the introduction in full to develop mental clarity.

Discussion Questions

1. What is a "move" in an introduction?
2. When is making more than one move helpful?
3. Should introductions be long or short?
4. Why are applications justified in introductions?

Recommended Reading

Awbrey, Ben. *How Effective Sermons Begin*. N.p.: Christian Focus Publications, 2008.

Merida, Tony. *Faithful Preaching*. Nashville: B&H, 2009.

Quicke, Michael J. *360-Degree Preaching: Hearing, Speaking, and Living the Word*. Grand Rapids: Baker Academic, 2001.

Ray, Jeff D. *Expository Preaching*. Whitefish: Kessinger, 2010.

Vines, Jerry, and Jim Shaddix. *Power in the Pulpit: How to Prepare and Deliver Expository Sermons*. Chicago: Moody, 1999.

11 | Thoughts on Delivery

Phillips Brooks famously said preaching is "truth through personality."[1] This quote has so embedded in the minds of a generation of preachers that for many, it is the *essence* of preaching. However, if misunderstood, it may lead to some dangerous places theologically. Brooks meant preaching takes the timeless truths of Scripture and communicates them in our own personality. He can be misunderstood to mean the text has no tone or personality of its own, and thus it must be supplied by the preacher. On the contrary, we preachers should not only preach the message of the text; we should preach the message of the text in the *personality* of the text.

Because the message of the text is shaped by the way it is communicated, the preacher must be sensitive to the message his delivery is communicating. Our chief consideration in the delivery of the text is not staying true to *our* personality, but rather staying true to the text's personality. Ultimately, the way a preacher delivers his sermon should not answer the question, "Who am I?" but rather, "What is the spirit of the text I am preaching?" Without a doubt, the preacher's personality will, and should, emerge. The problem is that most of us do not have big enough personalities to carry a sermon. A few preachers have such big personalities that they can overshadow the truth of the text. The liberating news is that even a preacher with an underwhelming

---

[1] Phillips Brooks, *The Joy of Preaching* (London: H. R. Allenson, 1895).

personality can be a compelling communicator of God's Word when he realizes delivery must be influenced by the tone of the text.

Jay E. Adams, author of more than 100 books, wrote that delivery must "grow out of and complement content at every point."[2] This is exactly the point. To take it one step further: *delivery is content in itself.* Yet we tend to distinguish between what we say and how we say it. We in the academy feed this misunderstanding because the sciences of hermeneutics (interpretation) and speech (communication) are distinct fields. However, simply put, there is substance in how something is said. Improper delivery can distort even the most basic truth. At its most innocent, improper delivery can make an astounding text seem lecture-dry. At its most dire, a text rich in truth can be delivered to serve the ego preaching it rather than the Creator it extols. While we want to be natural in the pulpit, the ultimate question of delivery is, "Did my approach to delivery accurately represent the message of the text?"

Our hope is to borrow the personality of the text and allow it to carry the sermon. There is so much more to say about sermon delivery that has been said in other places. This short chapter will be dedicated to preaching the spirit of the text and adding short words on the preacher's spiritual walk, and preaching without notes.

The Spirit of the Text

At this point in your sermon preparation, you will have outlined the structure of the text, determined how the author chose to shape his communication, and established what the substance of the text is—the actual content of the sermon. However, we have not discussed the spirit of the text. What is the spirit of the text? In short, it is *the author's intended emotional design of the text.* We might call it the text's *tone.*

---

[2] Jay E. Adams, *Pulpit Speech* (Grand Rapids: Baker, 1971), 130.

By this point in the preparation process, the spirit of the text may be clear. Clarity about the text's spirit is a natural consequence of the hours we spend grappling with it. As you determine the text's main idea, the thought, *OK, now, what is the spirit of the text?* may not ever occur to you. Still, the text's tone—its spirit—has likely become a part of you. You do not have to grapple with it the same way you did with the text's meaning. Simply put: as you study the text, you will understand its tone. Consider these examples.

Isaiah 1:18–20

The first chapter of Isaiah is a railing rebuke of Israel. God is so fed up that He wants His people to stop their religious practices altogether. However, He says,

> "Come, let us settle this,"
> says the LORD.
> "Though your sins are scarlet,
> they will be as white as snow;
> though they are crimson red,
> they will be like wool.
> If you are willing and obedient,
> you will eat the good things of the land.
> But if you refuse and rebel,
> you will be devoured by the sword."
> For the mouth of the LORD has spoken.

"Let's reason this out," He says. Though you have horribly disappointed God, He wants to forgive and restore you. The tone of the text is a stern warning followed by a promise, like a father rebuking his son with righteous anger and then reminding him their relationship is not wrecked forever, no matter how tenuous it may seem in the moment. Here's another example.

Psalm 103

> My soul, bless the LORD,
> and all that is within me, bless his holy name.
> My soul, bless the LORD,
> and do not forget all his benefits.
> He forgives all your iniquity;
> he heals all your diseases.
> He redeems your life from the Pit;
> he crowns you with faithful love and compassion.
> He satisfies you with good things;
> your youth is renewed like the eagle.

This is one of the most hopeful Psalms in all of Scripture. This text must be preached with hope and encouragement. The contrast between being in a pit and flying like an eagle could not be starker!

Genesis 3

This is a tragic story of disobedience and rebellion. It makes us want to weep. God's exact and perfect justice comes to reckon with Adam's sin. It is the ultimate tragedy: Adam has so broken his relationship with the perfect Father that he is asked to leave home. And yet, in the midst of this tragedy, there is a hint of redemption through one who will come and bruise the serpent's head.

James

The entire book of James is prophetic. Think of these commands:

> Consider it a great joy . . . whenever you experience various trials. (1:2)

> No one undergoing a trial should say, "I am being tempted by God." (1:13)

Don't be deceived. (1:16)

Don't criticize one another. (4:11)

In fact, there are more than 50 commands in this little epistle. There is no way to preach the book of James without a strong prophetic tone. (Remember that a prophet is simply one who shares the Word of God.)

When we preach, our individual personalities will inevitably emerge. However, our goal is to borrow the personality of the text.

The wife of a friend offered constructive criticism following one of his messages on the joys of heaven. After inquiring about his message, she told him, "The content of the message was great, but you looked angry as you preached on Heaven." His facial expressions mismatched the theme of the message, which detracted from the impact the message could have made. Make sure both your tone and your bearing match the tone of the text.

The Spiritual Walk of the Preacher

According to seminary professor Wayne McDill, the apostle Paul outlined expectations for the preacher in 1 Tim 4:12: "The preacher must have exemplary speech (*logos*) in and out of the pulpit, exemplary conduct (*anastrophe*) in every relationship of life, exemplary love (*agape*) as basic to Christian character, exemplary spirit (*pneuma*) in every attitude and expression, exemplary faith (*pistis*) for every challenge in ministry, exemplary purity (*hagneia*) without even the hint of sin."[3] When the man of God, empowered by the Spirit, preaches the Word of God appropriately, God's people will be edified and the Lord will be honored.

If you are a preacher and you are not spending daily time in God's Word, your preaching will suffer. We are called to preach out of the overflow of our devotional time with God. Someone rightly said, "I don't read the Bible to preach. I preach because I've read the Bible." The strongest

---

[3] Wayne V. McDill, *The Moment of Truth: A Guide to Effective Sermon Delivery* (Nashville: B&H, 1999), locs. 725–35, Kindle.

messages are those you live out daily before your people: You can't expect from others what you don't practice yourself. Of course, it is inevitable that some sermons you preach will require more obedience than you feel you have, almost as if you are preaching to yourself. Though you should not over-share personal failures, don't be afraid to admit your shortcomings before your congregation and commit to a deeper walk with Christ. John Poulton said, "The most effective preaching comes from those who embody the things they are saying."[4]

If the sermon doesn't move you during the week, it may not move your people on Sunday. Meditate on the text, pray through the text, and ask God to set you ablaze to preach the text. When the late pastor of Westminster Chapel D. Martyn Lloyd-Jones would preach, hearers would describe his sermons as "logic on fire."

On Preaching Without Notes

Notes are not required for effective preaching. Preaching without notes may seem impossible, but it's not. In fact, at the seminary where Steven teaches, they require students to preach without the use of notes. Some worry that preaching without notes will mean something gets left out. Certainly, that will happen. However, what may be lost in a thought or an illustration will be gained through deep connection with the audience.

If you do use some type of mental prompt, it must not be a distraction. This is why notes inside the Bible or on one page that does not have to be turned would be best. There are, of course, great preachers who use copious notes. But they are the exceptions. As a rule, to be compelling, we must look the congregation in the eye with a freedom from notes.

So how do you preach without notes? Here is some practical help.

---

[4] John Poulton, *A Today Sort of Evangelism* (n.p.: Lutterworth Press, 1972).

1. Know the text.

   An advantage of text-driven preaching is that every time you preach, you have a natural sermon outline in front of you: the text. You are not preaching a sermon, after all; you are preaching a text. The text becomes a part of you, and preaching is simply working it out.

2. Create a manuscript.

   This is a difficult process, but most helpful. Take all you have learned and write out the sermon word for word. This will not be read in the pulpit, and in fact, much of what you write will never make it to the pulpit. You are not trying to memorize the manuscript. Rather, the process of creating a written manuscript helps you develop a mental manuscript, which is really what you are after. Crafting detailed notes is one of the best ways not to need them.

3. Preach before you preach.

   Never preach a sermon for the first time. Before you walk into the pulpit, walk around your study, or take a walk outside, and preach through the sermon privately—either aloud or mentally. The reason is that when you are preaching, your mind is very active. This process will create fresh ideas and show you sections that need to be culled. Think of the confidence you experience when taking people on a journey you have already traveled. By preaching once privately, you are creating a mental manuscript to which you can return when you preach to the congregation.

Steven likes to prepare an outlined manuscript that he preaches through privately at least once, memorizing key transitions and sentences. Then he goes to the pulpit without any notes whatsoever: just a Bible.

I (Robby), on the other hand, bring a full manuscript to the platform each week, though I still employ the principles of the note-free technique. I do this for a few reasons:

1. Having a manuscript on the pulpit allows you to effortlessly recite quotes, statistics, and references, which I frequently do.

2. A preached-from manuscript can be repurposed into church emails, newspaper columns, blog posts, articles, books, and newsletters. I frequently amend manuscripts after I preach, either to update an illustration or to adjust a particular wording. Preaching from a manuscript helps me keep this process as streamlined as possible.

3. Finally, because I preach from a manuscript, I can share it with the tech crew, who will know exactly where I am in the sermon to follow along with digital media, such as quotes, sermon slides, and photographs.

Just because I have a manuscript with me does not mean I recite it as if I am reading a book though. Slumped posture, drooping shoulders, and monotone reading communicate a message to your audience, consciously or unconsciously, that detracts from the points you are trying to make. "Rather than practicing good gestures," commented McDill, "try to eliminate distracting ones."[5]

Eye contact is crucial for connecting with your audience. Your intentions and emotions are communicated through your eyes. Whether you use notes, a manuscript, or nothing at all, establishing eye contact with your audience builds rapport, opens communication, and expresses emotion. If you do choose to preach from a manuscript, take special care not to simply stand and read it. Research suggests that less than 50 percent eye contact in a message may communicate to the audience that you are "unfriendly, uninformed, inexperienced, and even dishonest."[6] Credibility is amplified through extended eye contact.

Not everyone will preach without notes. My encouragement is to preach without notes to prove to yourself you don't need them. Then back

---

[5] McDill, *The Moment of Truth*, locs. 1912–13.

[6] Steven A. Beebe and Susan J. Beebe, *Public Speaking Handbook*, 5th ed. (n.p.: Pearson, 2015), 233. McDill, *The Moment of Truth*, loc. 3630.

into an approach that works for you. There are no rules about preaching with or without notes, only principles. The main principle is this: establish eye contact with the audience and know your text well.

Discussion Questions

1. What is the "spirit" of the text, and how does it influence delivery?
2. What did Jay Adams mean when he said delivery must "grow out of and complement content at every point"?
3. What is the advantage of a full manuscript?
4. If you do not use a full manuscript, what should you at least put down on paper?

Recommended Reading

Adams, Jay. *Pulpit Speech*. Grand Rapids: Baker, 1971.

Brooks, Phillips. *The Joy of Preaching*. London: H. R. Allenson, 1895. Reprint, Grand Rapids: Kregel, 1989.

Fasol, Al. *A Complete Guide to Sermon Delivery*. Nashville: B&H, 1996.

Koller, Charles W. *How to Preach Without Notes*. Grand Rapids: Baker, 2007.

McDill, Wayne. *The 12 Essential Skills for Great Preaching*. Nashville: Broadman & Holman, 1994.

12 | Calling for Response

I (Robby) have devoted numerous pages and several years' worth of work to the merits of discipleship as Jesus practiced it. An often-overlooked aspect of such discipleship is the invitation. Jesus's discipleship relationships began after He extended the invitation to follow Him.

Remarkably, the same invitation to follow Christ is available today. How can we as preachers be intentional in calling people to action? How should a preacher extend an invitation? According to John R. W. Stott, "We must never issue an appeal without first making the proclamation. . . . People must grasp the truth before they are asked to respond to it."[1] Many are good at the first step: proclaiming the truth of Christ. But many preachers are uncertain about how to follow up: how to extend an invitation. In this chapter, we will examine various types of invitations, investigate how the invitation has been used throughout history, and then identify a system for extending an invitation biblically.

Invitation

Two forms of the invitation are found in the New Testament. "The first," according to professor of biblical exegesis R. Alan Streett in his book *The*

---

[1] John R. W. Stott, *The Preacher's Portrait: Five New Testament Word Studies* (Grand Rapids: Eerdmans, 1961; repr., n.p.: Langham, 2016), 28.

Effective Invitation, "called for sinners to demonstrate publicly their desire to repent and believe and was used as a means of bringing them to a state of conversion. The second called upon new converts, who had been supernaturally transformed by the message, openly to witness to their new-found faith."[2] The difference between these two forms is slight; they both constitute an evangelistic invitation.[3] An invitation can be extended for other decisions as well: baptism, church membership, and mission. However, in this chapter, we will focus on the appeal for salvation. At times, *invitation* will be used interchangeably with the terms *appeal, public pledge*, and *altar call.* While we will not spend much time discussing the specific form an invitation should take, any means of calling sinners to indicate publicly and immediately their desire to follow Christ falls within our definition of *invitation.* An altar call is perhaps the most obvious example of such an invitation, but the preacher is not limited to that format.

One of the first things to understand about the invitation is that human effort is not what draws people into a relationship with Jesus Christ. Streett elaborates on this idea: "Although the evangelistic preacher recognizes that most of his audience will reject his appeal, he persists in issuing an invitation, knowing that the Holy Spirit will take the universal call and turn it into a specific call for some."[4] Human teaching is not what changes an unbeliever's heart; rather, unbelievers are born again only through the divine work of the Holy Spirit.[5]

History of the Invitation

The Bible is filled with instances of the Lord calling people to respond to His Word publicly. Consider these instances of invitation:

---

[2] R. Alan Streett, *The Effective Invitation: A Practical Guide for the Pastor* (Grand Rapids: Kregel, 1984, 2004), 55.

[3] Salvation can and does take place outside of a public appeal issued by a preacher.

[4] Streett, *The Effective Invitation*, 242.

[5] See 2 Cor 2:6–16 and John 3:3–6.

God's invitation for Adam to step forward from hiding after disobeying His command to avoid the tree of the knowledge of good and evil (Gen 3:8–9).

God's invitation for Abraham to leave his comfortable surroundings for an unknown place, after which God fashioned a people for Himself (Gen 12:1–4).

Joshua's invitation for the people to turn from idols and return to Lord: "And if it is evil in your eyes to serve the LORD, choose this day whom you will serve, whether the gods your fathers served in the region beyond the River, or the gods of the Amorites in whose land you dwell. But as for me and my house, we will serve the LORD" (Josh 24:15 ESV).

Jesus's invitation at the beginning of His earthly ministry calling for repentance: "The time is fulfilled, and the kingdom of God is at hand; repent and believe in the gospel" (Mark 1:15 ESV). In another invitation, He said to would-be followers, "So everyone who acknowledges me before men, I also will acknowledge before my Father who is in heaven, but whoever denies me before men, I also will deny before my Father who is in heaven" (Matt 10:32–33 ESV).

Jesus's invitations for Zacchaeus to come down from the tree he had climbed and for Lazarus to come out of the tomb (Luke 19:1–10; John 11).

Each of these instances is an invitation following a proclamation of truth calling hearers to turn from old ways (of sin, of unbelief, of death) and toward the Lord. Scripture is filled with instances of people responding to the invitation to follow God.

Great Awakenings

Supporting the biblical model, history is filled with instances of men and women publicly responding to the gospel message. The Reformation-era Anabaptists were among the practitioners of the invitation. In his article "Invitations with Integrity," Mark Tolbert wrote, "The early Anabaptists helped bring a return to the use of the invitation. . . . They were faithful in calling for repentance of sins, faith in Christ, and the outward sign of believer's baptism."[6] At the conclusion of the proclamation of the Word, preachers invited unbelievers to repent and believe.

While instances of preachers' extending public invitations before the First and Second Great Awakenings are recorded, the practice was well documented beginning with this period.[7] Let us examine how God used such evangelists as Charles Finney, D. L. Moody, and Absalom B. Earle to deliver His message and employ what we now call the "classical invitation." Of these three, the most prominent advocate of invitations was Charles Finney. Finney disclosed the gospel with simplicity and clarity, making it easy for the hearer to respond to his message.[8]

In the early years of his ministry, Finney asked individuals to remain after the service for a time of consultation. As a result of the overwhelming response, he directed responders to small rooms in various buildings

---

[6] Mark Tolbert, "The Integrity of the Invitation," *Journal for Baptist Theology and Ministry* 6, vol. 2 (fall 2009): 92.

[7] David L. Allen and Steve W. Lemke, eds., *Whosoever Will* (Nashville: B&H, 2010), 242–44. Streett identified preachers who offered an invitation from the Roman Catholics (twelfth century), the Anabaptists (sixteenth century), and the Reformers (sixteenth and seventeenth centuries).

[8] Finney has been criticized for his theology and invitation tactics. Due to the scope of this chapter, these issues are not covered. However, we acknowledge the legitimacy of some critiques and hold up Finney as a role model in many respects without endorsing every aspect of his evangelistic methodology.

throughout the town. During his Rochester campaign of 1830, "inquirers were asked to come forward and occupy a front pew."[9]

In a comparable manner, Moody challenged unbelievers to respond to his message by standing to indicate a desire to be saved. Commenting on Moody's style, Charles Spurgeon noted, "I believe that it is a great help in bringing people to a decision when Mr. Moody asks those to stand who wish to be prayed for. Anything that tends to separate you from the ungodly around you is good for you."[10] Moody incorporated music during the invitation by recruiting Ira Sankey to lead worship for his revival meetings.[11] In an attempt to unite neighboring churches, Sankey contacted local music leaders to compile a choir to supplement his singing.

Baptist evangelist Absalom B. Earle popularized the use of commitment cards by calling people to sign a pledge at the end of the sermon. John Pollock outlined Earle's method: "Each person who came forward signed a card to indicate a pledge to live a Christian life and to show a church preference. This portion of the card was retained by the personal worker, so some type of follow-up could be worked out."[12]

Twentieth Century

From the beginning of Billy Graham's public ministry, his preferred ending to sermons was an invitation. Streett outlined the keys to Graham's effectiveness in delivering an invitation: a divine calling, a divine message, a

---

[9] Robert Lynn Asa, "The Theology and Methodology of Charles G. Finney as a Prototype for Modern Mass Evangelism" (PhD diss., Southern Baptist Theological Seminary, 1983), 205–6.

[10] Streett, *The Effective Invitation*, 97.

[11] Sankey left his government job to travel with Moody around the world. He understood the nature of crusade ministry since he was converted at 16 during a revival meeting at Kings Chapel Church.

[12] John Pollock, *Crusaders: Twenty Years with Billy Graham* (Minneapolis: World Wide, 1969), 8.

divine arsenal, and a divine enablement.[13] From the outset of the message, Graham called sinners to contemplate their position before a holy God: "He [Graham] consciously issues these initial appeals in an effort to prepare the people for the final call."[14]

During his ministry, Graham received criticism over his use of the invitation. In defense of the practice, he declared, "Some who are against public evangelistic invitations go to almost any length using the appeal in personal evangelism. If it is right to ask a single sinner to repent and receive the Lord Jesus Christ, why is it not right to ask a whole audience to do the same?"[15] His argument, in essence, was that since an individual gospel presentation ends with a call for repentance and faith, a corporate presentation should do the same.

Steps for Extending an Invitation

Many methods are available for extending a biblical invitation. A biblical invitation consists of four elements: transition, theological exhortation, persuasion, and reemphasis of the sermon's main idea.[16] Let's look at each:

Transition

A vital and often overlooked aspect of the invitation is the use of transitional statements to draw people to the Lord. An invitation linked to the

---

[13] Streett, *The Effective Invitation*, 121–30. Streett clarified the explanation to Graham's effectiveness: "Can charm, good looks, an all-American mystique, hypnotic eyes, or a seductive voice offer an adequate explanation? Obviously not" (122). Graham's ministry proved to be a divine work of God.

[14] Ibid., 116.

[15] O. S. Hawkins, *Drawing the Net: 30 Practical Principles for Leading Others to Christ Publicly and Personally* (Nashville: Broadman Press, 1993), 59. The author used the word *receive* interchangeably with the word *believe*.

[16] Streett identifies six elements in his book. Since the researcher assumed that the preacher prayed before preaching the sermon, this element was omitted from the study. Streett, *The Effective Invitation*.

end of a sermon with a smooth transition eliminates distractions inherent in a delayed approach. Many preachers are uncertain how to land the plane, so to speak, at the conclusion of the message. Steven Olford commented, "More sermons are ruined by a poor conclusion than for any other reason."[17] If the move from sermon body to invitation is disjointed or abrupt, the audience's attention can be diverted from the message of the text to the method of the messenger. Some telltale signs of disjointed movement to the invitation are phrases such as "As we close. . . ," "In conclusion . . . ," or "My final point . . ." At this point, Bibles close, notebooks are shut, and the audience disconnects and moves to the next item on their Sunday agendas.

Questions

One of the most effective ways to lead the audience into an engaging invitation is by asking enticing questions. The preacher does not craft clever questions, but rather "hears the questions playing on listeners' minds and then asks those questions *out loud*."[18]

This is a rabbinic technique Jesus used often when teaching.[19] While He did not use it as a method to transition between thoughts, He understood the power of inquiry as a method to teach particularly tricky concepts. In

---

[17] Stephen F. Olford, with David L Olford, *Anointed Expository Preaching* (Nashville: B&H Academic, 1998), 78.

[18] Ibid., 254, emphasis added.

[19] Dwight Pryor points out this literary device in his book *Behold the Man*. Luke 2 records the story of Jesus as a boy being left behind by His parents in Jerusalem after Passover, and His parents having to return to find Him. The text says, "After three days, they found him in the temple sitting among the teachers, *listening* to them and *asking* them questions. And all those who heard him were astounded at his understanding and his *answers*" (vv. 46–47; emphasis added). Jesus was listening and asking questions, but the sages of Israel were impressed with His answers. Pryor suggests, "Rabbis would engage a student by asking a question; the student would respond in kind with a related question, showing he understood what the rabbi was asking, and thereby advancing the discussion." Dwight A. Pryor, *Behold the Man* (Dayton: Center for Judaic-Christian Studies, 2005), 25.

the Gospels alone, He asked more than 100 questions.[20] More contemporarily, Billy Graham also employed appropriate, strategic questions planted throughout the sermon to set up an appeal for people to accept Jesus as their Lord and Savior.[21]

Transitional questions may bridge the gap for listeners who need a bit more help to make an essential, personal connection to the message. If you were preaching on Peter's confession in Matthew 16 that Jesus is the Messiah and the Son of God, you could rephrase the same question Jesus posed to the disciples: "Who do you say that Jesus is?" and then answer the question for them. "Jesus is the Christ, the Son of God. Have you settled that in your hearts today?"

Challenge

Challenging the congregation with an exhortation is another transitional technique. Staying with the example of Matthew 16, you may move to an invitation with a statement like this: "Knowing that Jesus is God's Son, sent for the redemption of your sins, *I urge you* today to repent of your sins and put your faith in Him." Simple, direct words will deliver your point with the most power; clarity of thought will make your transitional elements more dynamic. Sweazey grieves, "Too many sermons are static; they circle around the same idea so long that the congregation is begging, 'Let's go on with it.'"[22]

A challenge can come in the form of a choice between two alternatives, as seen in Joshua 24: "Therefore, fear the LORD and worship him in sincerity

---

[20] Bruce Demarest, *Who Is Jesus?: Further Reflections on Jesus Christ: The God-Man* (Eugene, OR: Wipf & Stock, 2007), 75.

[21] Streett, *The Effective Invitation*, 154.

[22] George Edgar Sweazey, *Preaching the Good News* (Englewood Cliff, NJ: Prentice-Hall, 1976), 76.

and truth. Get rid of the gods your fathers worshiped beyond the Euphrates River and in Egypt, and worship the LORD. But if it doesn't please you to worship the LORD, choose for yourselves today: Which will you worship— the gods your fathers worshiped beyond the Euphrates River or the gods of the Amorites in whose land you are living?" (vv. 14–15).

Movement and Space

Certain aspects of your physical presence can help you transition into a time of invitation. Frequently, physical transition cues are used in conjunction with other techniques. The preacher can physically insert a transitional device by changing his stance or position. If he normally preaches from behind a pulpit with his hands on either side of it, he may walk to the front of the stage and slip his hands into his pockets as he moves into the invitation. This signals to listeners that a new phase of the sermon is beginning.

Theological Exhortation

Don't assume your listeners understand the "next steps" for responding to the message you just preached. Connect the dots for them by explaining exactly how you expect them to respond. If the message is about salvation, instruct them to repent and believe. If the message is about prayer, suggest specific ways to foster healthy conversation with God. If the message is about purity, disclose ways to intentionally walk in holiness.

Consider this: When people don't know what to do, they don't do anything at all. Conversely, when people have too many options, they don't do anything at all. This is called *analysis paralysis*. Therefore, make your final instructions brief and simple. Clear instructions guide the hearers in responding to the message. What's more, every evangelistic invitation must exhort the hearers to respond in two ways: repentance and faith.

Repentance

Repentance carries the meaning of the Old Testament word *teshuva,* which means "to go back again or to return."[23] It means to change one's mind about something or to change one's direction. The prophets used this word as a call to return to God. "A reversal of one's thinking," according to Roland Q. Leavell, ". . . will result in an alteration of one's way of living."[24] Repentance is found in two forms in the Bible: repentance unto salvation—starting a relationship with Christ; and repentance unto sanctification—continuing a relationship with Christ.[25] "The first call the gospel preacher must give in his invitation," declared Streett, "is that of repentance."[26]

Faith

Faith is confidence that something is true, based on the evidence you have been presented. The verb form of *faith* is used 242 times in the New Testament. The Greek word for faith, *pistis,* can be translated as "belief," "trust," or "reliance upon someone or something." *The Greek-English Lexicon of the New Testament* defines faith as "considering something to be true and therefore worthy of one's trust."[27] In other words, faith is believing something is true and then letting that belief affect your life in

---

[23] Francis Brown, Samuel Rolles Driver, and Charles Augustus Briggs, *Enhanced Brown-Driver-Briggs Hebrew and English Lexicon,* electronic ed. (Oak Harbor, WA: Logos Research Systems, 2000), 996.

[24] Quoted in Streett, *The Effective Invitation,* 42.

[25] Paul explained repentance in 1 Thess 1:9.

[26] Streett, *The Effective Invitation,* 43.

[27] William Arndt, Frederick W. Danker, and Walter Bauer, *A Greek-English Lexicon of the New Testament and Other Early Christian Literature,* 3rd ed. (Chicago: University of Chicago Press, 2000), 816.

a drastic, permanent way. In an evangelistic sermon, the goal is to present the good news of Jesus Christ's death, resurrection, and ascension as the object of faith.

Persuasion

The preacher's words do not save a person. However, it is his duty to make a clear and poignant case for putting one's faith in Jesus Christ. For some, explanation and instruction alone may be insufficient motivation to respond to an invitation to follow Christ. For this reason, the preacher should persuade the hearers to respond. The apostle Paul, highlighting the motivation behind his ministry, told the Corinthian church, "Therefore, since we know the fear of the Lord, we try to persuade people" (2 Cor 5:11). The preacher can personalize the invitation by speaking directly to the hearers. Using personal pronouns such as *you* and *your* in place of *they* and *them* concentrates on the person rather than the group and aids persuasion.

The Main Idea

An expository preacher will weave the central theme of the text throughout the sermon and include it, in fully developed form, in the invitation. The invitation is an extension of this central theme of the message. It cannot be a new point all on its own, for a new concept at this point—one that was not addressed in the body of the message—disconnects the message from the invitation.

Building the invitation around the sermon's main idea develops continuity toward the invitation. Among ways to repeat the main idea during the invitation are illustrations from the Bible (perhaps parables) and illustrations from contemporary life.[28] The invitation should conclude a strain of thought that began in the introduction.

---

[28] Ibid., 162.

Begin with the End in Mind

The invitation at the conclusion of a message should be the overwhelming culmination of truth from God's Word, not a forced reaction or a guilt trip. It is more than just a call for salvation; it's also a call for response to the truths heard throughout the message. It should be the logical, natural end of the points made.

Because we expect lost people to be in attendance at every sermon, the greatest necessity in an invitation is a focus on repentance and faith. A focused invitation will clear up ambiguity for unbelievers in the congregation and solidify truths that believers already know. Every element of the sermon should point toward the need for and sufficiency of repenting and believing in Christ.

In addition to calling for repentance and faith, preachers should present a clear explanation of the gospel at the conclusion of the message. Streett suggests explaining the death, burial, and resurrection of Christ as a means for transitioning into the invitation. Although the message of the gospel is not mentioned in every passage of Scripture, the preacher can highlight the importance of the gospel before issuing a challenge to respond with repentance and faith.

Finally, an effective invitation happens when the theme of the sermon matches the theme of the invitation. The invitation calls the congregation to action based on what you told them in the sermon. (Appendix 1 contains a helpful tool for evaluating an invitation.)

Preaching from the Rest in Us

Text-driven preaching, this preaching for the rest of us, is preaching *from* the rest in us. This is because preaching, text-driven preaching, is a great act of humility. It begins with our call to ministry: We bow before the Father when He calls us. We bow before the Word when we study each week. We humble ourselves under the structure, substance, and spirit of the text when we prepare sermons that are driven by the text and not our own ideas.

The ambitions of this book are summed up in Jesus's parable of the farmer of Mark 4:26–29:

> And he said, "The kingdom of God is as if a man should scatter seed on the ground. He sleeps and rises night and day, and the seed sprouts and grows; he knows not how. The earth produces by itself, first the blade, then the ear, then the full grain in the ear. But when the grain is ripe, at once he puts in the sickle, because the harvest has come."

The farmer sows the seed, and then he goes to sleep. He rests. Why? Because "the earth produces by itself" (v. 28). How all this happens, he doesn't know. He just knows that it does. He can rest. The act of preaching is deferring to the law of kingdom harvest. We know that the kingdom will produce fruit, even if we don't know how or when it will happen. It's an act of faith birthed in confidence in God's Word. We sow the seed with great effort and then rest in the power of His Word. So again, in the end, preaching for the rest of us is preaching *from* the rest in us, forged from a steely confidence in Scripture.

APPENDIX 1
SERMON ANALYSIS TOOL

Sermon Information

Preacher:

Sermon Title:

Text:

Date Preached:

Place Preached:

Sermon Analysis

I. Preparation of the Invitation

A. Transitions

1. Did the preacher use connective questions?

2. Did the preacher offer a challenge to the audience? If so, what were the hearers challenged to do?

3. Did the preacher give the audience a choice? If so, what were the options given?

4. Did the preacher explain a promise from the Word? If so, what was the promise?

B. Theological Instructions

1. Did the preacher instruct the hearers to repent?

    a. Were illustrations used to explain the term?

    b. Was biblical evidence incorporated?

2. Did the preacher instruct the hearers to believe?

    a. Were illustrations used to explain the term?

    b. Was biblical evidence incorporated?

3. Did the preacher instruct the hearers to follow Christ?

    a. Were illustrations used to explain the concept?

    b. Was biblical evidence incorporated?

4. What were the preacher's final remarks to the congregation?

C. Persuasion

1. Was persuasion used? If yes, how so?

2. Was the invitation personal?

D. Main Idea

1. What was the theme of the invitation?

2. Did the theme match the central theme of the message?

II. Comments

APPENDIX 2
RECOMMENDED NEXT STEPS

A Summary of Steps to Crafting a Text-Driven Sermon

Chapter 3: The Frame of the Text

1. Read the text 20 times.
2. Identify the structure of the text and express it with a diagram.
3. Craft the first draft of a textual idea.

Chapter 4: Exegesis of the Text

Create an exegetical outline. This is an outline of the text that notes the structure, the textual idea, and all of your exegetical work. It may have references to commentaries, quotations, and so on. It will have many things that will not make the final cut, but that's OK. This is simply the process of information gathering.

Chapter 5: The External Frame

Take your text and zoom out by reading the whole chapter, determining its context in the book, and researching how this text fits into the larger picture of Scripture.

Chapter 6: Translation

1. Translate the exegetical outline into a communication outline.
2. Translate the textual idea into a main idea.

Chapter 7: Explanation

1. Write out the explanation proper for each point.
2. Include any argumentation needed within the explanation.
3. Write out the illustration for each point.

Chapter 8: Exhortation

Develop application from the text and decide where to place it within the body of the sermon. This may take place within the points of the sermon, or it may take place all at the end of the sermon. As we think through the application, we ask these questions: Does the spirit of the application carry with it a tone of exhortation? Am I both giving practical help and compelling listeners to bring their lives into conformity with God's Word? Once this is done, the bulk of the sermon is complete.

Chapter 9: Conclusions

Develop a conclusion built around one move that will reinforce one main idea. Whether you choose to type or handwrite your full sermons or not, it is advisable that you always do so with the conclusion and the introduction. Having the introduction and the conclusion before you in manuscript form keeps them crisply in your mind and is the best way to enter the pulpit with confidence.

Chapter 10: Introductions

Locate the question the text is raising. Assume this will be the last sentence of the introduction. Then, cultivate a "move" that will get the listener to that question. Employ one or two moves, state the question the text is raising, and then move on to the exposition proper. Now write out the introduction in full in order to develop mental clarity.

Chapter 11: Thoughts on Delivery

Exegete the tone of the text. What tone did the author use? What kind of message is this? Where is the warning? Where is the hope? Match the tone of your voice to the tone of the text while preaching the sermon.

Write your manuscript. Your exegesis is complete. You have studied the text. You know it thoroughly. You've constructed a main idea. You have written down pertinent illustrations, applications, arguments, and exhortations. Now, write your manuscript. You may not take it to the pulpit. The manuscript is for your benefit during the preparation stage. Write for the ear, not the eye. Each sentence in your manuscript will typically be between eight and twelve words.

Internalize the message. You are not ready to preach a sermon until the sermon has been internalized. Think through your manuscript—from start to finish. Work through each point and/or scene. Know your transitions. Practice it repeatedly. Make the functional elements of the sermon crisp. Although you will not memorize your manuscript, there is no word or phrase in your sermon that should catch you by surprise when you preach.

APPENDIX 3
GLOSSARY

deductive sermon structure. A sermon that develops a text by moving from an idea.

didactic text. A text that teaches a particular truth in a non-imperatival way.

exegetical outline. An outline of the text that has the structure, the textual idea, and the preacher's exegetical work.

expositional epistle. A text that teaches one particular theological truth.

genre. A literary vehicle used to communicate a point in a certain style. There are arguably nine discernible genres in Scripture.

hortatory texts. Texts that give commands.

inductive sermon structure. A sermon that develops a text by moving toward an idea.

interpretation. The process that seeks to answer the question, what does this text mean?

main idea. The subject and complement of a sermon's central thought.

narrative texts. Texts that unfold like a story.

panning out. An interpretive investigation whereby the reader discovers the meaning of a text and how that text is framed in the broader scope of a chapter, book, and the whole of Scripture, and bringing that meaning to bear on the individual text.

parallelism. A literary technique in Hebrew poetry in which what is stated is either reinforced, explained, or contrasted in the subsequent line.

pericope. A complete unit of thought.

procedural texts. Texts that lay out certain protocols.

spirit. The biblical author's intended emotional design of a text.

strophe. A contained unit of thought in Hebrew poetry that functions like a verse in a song.

structure. The biblical author's semantic outline of a text.

substance. The content of a sermon that proceeds from a biblical text.

text-driven preaching. The interpretation and communication of a biblical text in a sermon that reflects the structure, substance, and spirit of the text.

zooming in. An interpretive investigation whereby readers seek to discover the internal frame of a text.

APPENDIX 4

DISCUSSION QUESTIONS

Chapter 1: A Theology of Text-Driven Preaching

1. If the Word is the agent used by the Holy Spirit for sanctification, how does this impact our view of Scripture and, ultimately, our view of a theology of preaching?
2. Text-driven preaching is a philosophy that emanates from a high view of Scripture. How does this philosophy of preaching influence our method of preaching?
3. Read Luke 24:27. Luke records Jesus revealing Himself through the Old Testament Scriptures. How does this verse, specifically, impact a theology of preaching?
4. The preacher dies so that others may live. How does this manifest itself on a week-to-week basis for preachers?

Chapter 2: What Is Text-Driven Preaching?

1. A text-driven sermon reflects the structure of the biblical text. Explain the difference between slavishly copying the structure of the text in a sermon and allowing the text's structure to inform the sermon.

2. Consider the definition given for text-driven preaching. It is "the interpretation and communication of a biblical text in a sermon that represents the substance, structure, and spirit of the text." How does the preacher determine the author's spirit, or emotive design, of the text?

3. What does it mean to zoom in or to pan out?

4. Why is it necessary to zoom in and pan out in the interpretive process?

Chapter 3: The Frame of the Text

1. Generally speaking, when handling a narrative text, should the preacher work from a point (deductive approach) or work to a point (inductive approach)?

2. Generally speaking, when handling an epistle, should the preacher work from a point (deductive approach) or work to a point (inductive approach)?

3. Define *strophe*. How does the strophic structure in poetry impact the way an expositor preaches Wisdom literature?

4. What is the primary motivation for understanding the structure of a text? See page 53.

5. How does the preacher let the text breathe? Should the questions raised in the sermon stem from the mind of the preacher or the biblical text? Why is text-driven preaching elevated above therapeutic preaching and doctrinal preaching?

Chapter 4: Exegesis of the Text

1. Preaching is working out of you what God has worked into you. How, then, does the preacher allow God to work into him?

2. When preaching an epistle, what is the difference between hortatory, procedural, expositional, and didactic genre?

3. What is the proper length of text when preaching a narrative?

4. In the process of sermon preparation, when should a preacher consult a commentary?

5. When handling a narrative text, should a preacher use "points" or "themes?" Why?

Chapter 5: The External Frame

1. Why is it necessary for the preacher to zoom out of the immediate context and consider the surrounding context, book context, and canonical context?

2. What is one benefit of preaching sequentially through books of the Bible?

3. Explain the relationship between the divine Author and the human authors of Scripture.

4. A fourfold outline of Scripture was given in this chapter. Can you identify the four macro sections?

5. When preaching the Old Testament, is it hermeneutically responsible for the preacher to interpret forward from the Old Testament to the New Testament?

Chapter 6: Translation

1. Define the "exegetical idea" and the sermon's "main idea." What are the similarities and differences?

2. The metaphor of a deep-sea diver was given in this chapter. What do we mean by to "sink," to "surface," and to "shine"?

3. How will the textual divisions differ from the communication divisions when considering different genres of Scripture?

4. How does a textual outline differ from a communication outline?

5. According to this chapter, what might be the greatest homiletical challenge for preachers?

Chapter 7: Explanation

1. Explaining a text has three components. Can you name each one?
2. Four helps for crafting the explanation were given in this chapter. Can you name them?
3. When should a preacher use personal illustrations?
4. Where can you find good illustrations?
5. What is the purpose of argumentation in preaching? Does argumentation incite boredom or benefit the preacher? Why?

Chapter 8: Exhortation

1. Should application come at the exclusion of exhortation? Why or why not? If not, what is the connection between application and exhortation?
2. How can the preacher's desire for exegetical accuracy at times mute his prophetic voice?
3. How does a preacher put application in its correct place?
4. How does the genre of the text impact where the preacher places application in the sermon?
5. How should the preacher weave illustration and application?

Chapter 9: Conclusions

1. How long should a conclusion be?
2. Should the conclusion always end with a story?
3. Should the conclusion drive home the point of the whole sermon, or just the last point?
4. Should the conclusion include ways to respond? Why or why not?
5. Is it advisable to "bookend" the sermon by completing a story line that surfaced in the introduction?

Chapter 10: Introductions

1. What is a "move" in an introduction?
2. When is making more than one move helpful?
3. Should introductions be long or short?
4. Why are applications justified in introductions?

Chapter 11: Thoughts on Delivery

1. What is the "spirit" of the text, and how does it influence delivery?
2. What did Jay Adams mean when he said delivery must "grow out of and complement content at every point"?
3. What is the advantage of a full manuscript?
4. If you do not use a full manuscript, what should you at least put down on paper?

Name Index

Subject Index

Scripture Index